Adolf Galland

A PILOT'S LIFE IN WAR AND PEACE

Adolf Galland

A PILOT'S LIFE
IN WAR AND PEACE

By Werner Held
Additional material by Anton Weiler

Champlin Museum Press
Mesa, Arizona

Reprinted by permission of Podzun-Pallas Verlag GMBH 6360
Friedberg 3 • Markt 9 • Postfach 314 • West Germany

English language rights held by Champlin Fighter Museum Press

International Standard Book Number 0-912173-08-4
Printed in the United States of America

Library of Congress Cataloging in Publication Data

Held, Werner -
Adolf Galland: A Pilot's Life

Translation of: Adolf Galland.
1. Galland, Adolf, 1912-. 2. Fighter Pilots — Germany — Biography. I. Weiler, Anton. II. Title.
UG626.2.G35H4513 1986 358.4'14'0924 [B] 86-9759

Contents

Acknowledgments

Many individuals helped bring this volume to completion in English. Herr Ahnert of Podzun-Pallas Verlag co-ordinated with General Galland in Germany. The text of Werner Held and Anton Weiler was translated by Sergei Sikorsky, as were the photo captions, over a six-month period.

The various photographs came from widespread sources in the original German edition, and they have been reproduced here. In addition to General Galland's extensive collection, the following individuals and organizations provided much assistance: Herr Bode, Herr Christl, Herr Emmert, Herr Geisinger, Herr Geyer, Herr Happ, Herr Haugk, Herr Schmitz, Herr Schopfel, Herr Neumann, Herr Siebeck and Herr Weiler; Foto B-Studio and the U.S. Air Force.

Data for the text was obtained in part from: *Jagerblatt*, the publication of the German Fighter Pilot's Association; Galland's own *The First and the Last;* Ernst Obermaier's *Die Ritterkreuztrager der Luftwaffe;* and Josef "Pips" Priller's monumental history of Jagdgeschwader 26.

Finally, a warm word of thanks and appreciation to Dolfo and Heidi Galland for their participation. Getting to know them as friends has been a rewarding experience for everyone at the Champlin Fighter Museum. If this volume contains a message, it is found in Werner Held's introduction: the quality of the man may be seen in the number of his friends.

Barrett Tillman
Publisher
Champlin Museum Press

Introduction

The preparation of this book started in May of 1978. Some five years of effort were required before the book was finally published. It records the life of a personality who, still today, is frequently mentioned in the press and in TV interviews: Adolf Galland.

During the five years I was occupied with this book, I grew to know and appreciate Galland as a human being. He was always at my disposal, helping me with endless patience, but also, with steady determination, pushing and supporting me to complete the work. I hope that I was able to capture some of the unique facets of his life.

Even in the early days of World War II, the name Galland was already linked to a reputation for fairness and chivalry. Those characteristics established his name and today, over 40 years later, the quality of that man can be seen in the number of friends he has.

I wish Adolf Galland many more peaceful years. He, together with his many friends, will continue with the task of building greater understanding among people in a future blessed with peace and freedom.

Werner Held
August 1983

Foreword

This book provides an accurate and splendid record of Adolf Galland who, in my opinion, was Germany's greatest fighter pilot and leader in World War II. It is an honest account of events as Galland saw and experienced them. The disastrous political decisions which were made by the Fuhrerhauptqartier plus the tactical stupidities of Reich Marshal Goering, are clearly identified.

Galland and I must have first met in the sky over England in August/September 1940, although at that time we would not have recognised each other. During the first year of World War II, both the Luftwaffe and the R.A.F. got to know the names of individual pilots opposing them. Galland and Molders were the two outstanding German names which drifted across our side of the Channel. I met Galland physicially for the first time in August 1941, when I was brought down on his side. He and his pilots entertained me most courteously when I was in hospital at St. Omer. At the end of the war in 1945, I was able to return his hospitality when we entertained him and some other German pilots at Tangmere, Sussex.

This book is not only about war, although Galland's name will forever be famous as a result of it. Like many others who fought for their country during those memorable six years, there was much of his life left after the war. It is all fascinatingly told in this book. I am happy to say that our first postwar meeting in June 1945, was the start of a continuing friendship, which will last our lifetime. Apart from meeting privately in my house with other friends, we have been together at various Wartime Pilots Reunions. I well remember the first of such meetings in September 1970, in Winnipeg in

Douglas Bader

Canada, when Galland, the great Canadian pilot Fauquier, Johnson and I were the guests of honour. At the end of the lunch, the Mayor of Winnipeg presented the Freedom of the City to the four of us. I was sitting next to Dolfo and when he received his award, I muttered to him, "I cannot think what you have done for the City of Winnipeg!"

This is a fine book, which should be in the library of every aviation enthusiast. It is an accurate historical record of the life and times of a great German patriot. Politicians cause wars and the ordinary decent citizen fights them. The true fighting man bears no animosity towards his opponent, in whom he recognizes the same attitude of mind as his own. When such men meet subsequently, it is understandable that they will become friends.

Douglas Bader
London 1979

Adolf Galland

A PILOT'S LIFE
IN WAR AND PEACE

From Glider to Jet Pilot

"Flying is more than a sport and more than a job; flying is pure passion and desire, which fill a lifetime".
A.G. ***The First and the Last***

These words truly say everything about Adolf Galland. The great passion of his life was, and continues to be, aviation. As a young boy, it became part of him and has not released him even today. This fascination started almost like a game, soaring silently in the wind and clouds and ended in April 1945 flying the Me-262, the world's first operational jet fighter. He followed his passion consistently even in those years when everything seemed hopeless, and he survived by his inner strength.

Political developments in the early 1930s offered the youth of Germany the opportunity to take to the air. The young aviation enthusiast cannot be blamed for the fact that those same politics led directly to the cruelties of WW II. Most of the same youngsters who took to the air so enthusiastically paid for it with their lives later on.

Adolf Galland lived in and survived those serious, deadly years. He was able to reach the top of the ladder within a few years, and then had to start over again following the end of the war. Having lived through many bitter experiences without having them affect him, he started to rebuild his life. Again he chose his first love, aviation. Probably he could not have chosen any other career. The nature of his personality and his open-mindedness allowed him to turn many of his former enemies into his closest personal friends. His dynamic personality, well known and appreciated throughout the world, has helped this process.

His fairness, not only when he was winning, but also at a time when one defeat followed another, became an example for others. If it is true that the value of a human being can be measured in his friends, Adolf Galland can stand comparison with any other figure of that period.

As a youth, Galland gained his first experience of gliding near his home in the Borkenberge Hills in Westphalia in north-central Germany.

By the age of 17 he had the A-and-B glider ratings. Two years later he obtained the "C" at the famed Wasserkuppe gliding center in the Rhon Valley. In that same year, 1931, he was awarded a formal glider license which allowed him to fly high performance sail planes cross-country. He barely squeezed through the University Entrance Examination in 1932 and was presented by his family with his own glider as a reward.

On 27 February 1932, Galland established a soaring record of more than two hours in his Grunau-Baby I, nicknamed *Strolch.* This record in the Borkenberge Hills qualified the area as an official gliding center. He then entered the transport pilot training school at Braunschweig and, after graduation, was sent to basic military training with an infantry regiment in Dresden. At the end of 1934 he graduated as a lieutenant of infantry from the Dresden officers' academy and returned to aviation, this time at Schleissheim. This air training academy, a disguised fighter pilot training school, gave Galland much valuable experience. In March 1935, the Luftwaffe was officially unveiled and he was assigned to Fighter Wing 2 *Richthofen* at Doberitz, near Berlin. This wing was the cradle of many fighter wings to follow.

As commander of an observation squadron - which carried a Mickey Mouse emblem as its insignia - Galland gained valuable experience during the Spanish Civil War. His knowledge of close air support became of great value during the Polish campaign in 1939 and the "Blitz" of 1940.

During the lightning war against Poland, Galland was promoted to first lieutenant and commander of Close Air Support Squadron 4. After the Polish campaign, his continuous efforts to be reassigned to fighters bore fruit and he became operations officer of Fighter Wing 27 on the French/Belgian coast.

On 10 June 1940, after scoring his twelfth aerial victory, Captain Galland was transferred to Fighter Wing 26 as commander of its third squadron. He was promoted to major on 18 July of the same year; after his 17th air victory and many low-level attack missions, he was awarded the Knight's Cross to the Iron Cross on 1 August 1940.

That same August, many new responsibilities suddenly appeared. The command structure of the fighter wings, largely composed of World War I veterans, was gradually replaced by younger fighter pilots. Galland was promoted to commander of Fighter Wing 26. In addition to the strain of daily air combat missions, a heavy administrative load was thrust upon him. How Galland rapidly mastered these new responsibilities was documented in "Pips" Prillers' outstanding book, *The History of Fighter Wing 26.* The wing rapidly earned the reputation of being . . . "a tough unit, led by a tough commander, operating against a tough enemy." Priller commented that Galland was an officer always ready for combat, an aggressive and unusually capable pilot and marksman; equally good in split-second decisions and reactions.

During those brief periods when he was not leading his wing on missions, Galland's administrative and organizational talents were even further developed. As the Armed Forces Daily Communiques carried his name with increasing frequency, the fighter pilot with the mustache and cigar became nearly as well known as Germany's leading fighter ace, Major Molders. After his 40th victory in September 1940, Galland was awarded the Oak Leaves to the Knight's Cross, only the third soldier to receive this decoration. After his 69th aerial victory, he became the first German soldier awarded the crossed swords to the Knight's Cross, on 21 June 1941. That was the unforgettable day he shot down three fighters and was himself shot down twice.

In November of 1941, Colonel Molders was killed in a crash during a flight from the Russian front to Berlin. Galland was promoted to colonel and nominated Commander of the German Day Fighter Arm. The promotion resulted in his leaving JG-26 to inspect the fighter wings on various fronts. During these visits, Galland gathered much valuable information regarding operational conditions and the problems encountered by the Luftwaffe.

His 94 aerial victories on the Western front earned Galland the Knight's Cross with diamonds on 28 January of 1942. The spectacular "Channel Dash" of the German battleships, 12 and 13 February 1942, was supported by very successful cooperation between the Navy and the Luftwaffe. Galland personally organized and directed the control of the air space over the battleship formation as it steamed through the English Channel.

In the following months, Galland continued visiting his fighter units. Hitler, who had declared in 1940 that he would avoid a second front, now created a third theater of war, North Africa, in addition to the European and Russian fronts. The Luftwaffe began to be stretched thinner and thinner.

Ernst Udet, before he committed suicide, had said, "If we cannot reinforce the fighter arm and gain a victory by the end of 1942... we have lost the war". The replacement of lost pilots and damaged aircraft, and the constant dilution of units grew into critical problems. On 19 November 1942 Galland was promoted once again, becoming the youngest general in the German Armed Forces. He was at that time 30 years old.

1943 marked increasingly heavy attacks on German cities and industry, as American forces began their massive buid-up in Europe. The highest priority was assigned to the manufacture of both day and night-fighters. General Galland had demanded more (and better-trained) fighter pilots and increased aircraft production, but the German High Command was slow to react, However, by May of 1943 fighter production reached 900 units; in the following months production increased to 1,000 fighters monthly. A large portion of these were being diverted from air defense to close air support and reconnaissance. Galland flew the Me-262 jet fighter on 22 May 1943. The hope of receiving this superior fighter was dashed to pieces when Hitler made his well-known decision to assign this outstanding aircraft to "Blitz Bomber" duties. This decision delayed introduction of the Me-262 by one irreplaceable year. Despite the fact that new fighter wings were steadily being organized and a special effort was made to increase night-fighter capabilities, the devastating night attacks on Hamburg and other German cities confirmed the basic weakness of Night Fighter Command. In late 1943 Galland was assigned responsibility for the Night Fighters as well, and literally needed 24 hours of working time per day. While continuously inspecting fighter units, he visited the various aircraft design offices. His professional knowledge and experience were always well received. He was also kept abreast of progress at the various test centers which were developing a series of new weapons and aircraft designed to regain some measure of air superiority over Germany.

Friction between Reich Marshal Goring and "his" fighter force was rapidly increasing. Goring had blamed the fighter pilots for the destruction caused by allied air raids. He accused them of lacking courage and aggressiveness. However, he was neither willing nor able to communicate with Hitler in an effort to resolve their problems. During a violent argument, in the presence of several officers, Goring repeated the accusations to Galland, who ripped his Knight's Cross from his own neck and demonstratively threw it on the table in front of a shocked Goring. Galland refused to wear any decorations for some time after that episode, as a protest.

In the summer of 1944, Goring was finally able to convince Hitler to allow the organization of the first Me-262 fighter unit. Galland chose an outstanding fighter pilot, Major Walter Nowotny, to command this unit.

After some initial dificulties, the success of Nowotny's jet fighter unit was so spectacular that it convinced Hitler to authorize the organization of the first jet fighter wing, JG-7.

However, the decision was far too late. German cities and industries were largely destroyed. The complex fuel refineries were devastated.

The moderate success of the fighters, accomplished despite enormous losses, could no longer have any effect. After Galland was relieved as fighter commander in January of 1945, Hitler cancelled his earlier order forbidding Galland to fly in combat. The young general was directed to set up "Fighter Unit Galland". Former squadron leaders and pilots, in disgrace because of the "fighter pilots mutiny" (or a number of other reasons), flocked to new Fighter Unit 44. These, the so-called "experts," checked out on the legendary Me-262 and flew their last missions from Munich-Riem airfield.

They were not ordered to fly, but fought as volunteers. Although they knew that the outcome of the war was already decided, they could not resist the challenge to fly this new aircraft in combat.

On 26 April 1945, after his two final air victories, Galland was wounded. Following discharge from the military hospital at Tegernsee, he surrendered himself to the U.S. troops and became a prisoner of war for two years.

The Galland family home in Westerholt/Westfalia. Adolf Galland, the second of four sons, was born here: Fritz (21 May 1910), Adolf (19 March 1912), Wilhelm-Ferdinand (23 October 1914) and Paul (3 November 1919) spent their childhood years here.

The parents, Adolf and Anne Galland. The father was administrator and estate manager of the Earl of Westerholt. For some 200 years this title had been transferred from the father to one of his sons. The first Galland, a Hugenotte, fled from France to Germany in 1742.

Many years ago: The five-year-old Adolf (1917).

First gliding lessons in the Borkenberge. The flying club of Gelsenkirchen rented this area from the Earl of Westerholt for use as a gliding training area. Here Adolf Galland learned gliding from the ground up; a lot of theory, many hours in the workshop, and during the weekends, actual flying with all the resulting hard work. Galland is second from left; next to him his friend and instructor Theo Keweloh.

Under the qualified direction of instructor George Ismer, this aerodynamically improved version of the Zogling training glider was among the many built in the Vocational High School at Gelsenkirchen.
The constructors proudly show the result of many hours in the workshop. In row three, third from the left is Adolf Galland; next to him, Theo Keweloh.

In 1929, the 17-year-old Galland successfully passed the A and B gliding tests during a training course in Borkenberge. The photo shows Adolf before a take-off in a *Falke*.

Easter vacation of 1931 was spent at the Wassakuppe in the Rhon. After a ten-minute soaring flight with the Falke, Galland earned the C-class insignia. In the autumn of 1931 he earned the official glider pilot certificate on the same hill.

On February 11 and 12th, 1932 Adolf Galland graduated from the Hindenburg High School in Buer. In his certificate it was noted, "Galland wants to be a pilot." The outlines of his professional career are emerging.

Members of the "Gelsenkirchen Luftsportverein" in front of the Mayer II glider in the Borkenberge. Adolf Galland stands next to the fuselage and to his left his instructor and friend, Theo Keweloh.

As a graduation present, Galland got his own glider. Before the first take-off Galland checks the control cables of his Grunau *Baby I*. In the left foreground, Galland's father watches his son. On 27 February 1932, Galland established a local record of two hours, six minutes and five seconds. This flight qualified Borkenberge as an official gliding site.

In early 1932, Galland was admitted to the *Deutsche Verkehrsfliegerschule* (DVS), German Airlines School. He was one of 20 lucky persons selected from roughly 4,000 applicants.
Trainee Galland with Stutz, his first instructor, before takeoff in an Albatross L 101. The smaller photo shows Galland after a cross-country flight from Braunschweig to Konigsberg in an Albatross L 75 *Ace*.

Galland prefers this photograph of him as a "flight student on duty" at the DVS Braunschweig in 1932, as it shows his classical nose which later suffered from several accidents and was transformed into one of his trademarks.

As a prerequisite to beginning an officer's career, the young pilots had to complete basic military training. On 15 February 1934, Galland was transferred to Infantry Regiment 10 in Dresden for basic training. In the photograph, Galland during a cross-country march in a relaxed formation.

After completing basic training the process continued at the Military Academy in Dresden. Besides infantry-officer training the young men also were tought air tactical operations. The photo shows the officer cadets with their instructor in the center. Cadet Galland is third from the left in the front row. In late 1934, Galland was promoted to second lieutenant and returned to active flying - this time to Schleissheim near Munich.

At this branch of the DVS - actually an "underground" fighter pilot's school of the future Luftwaffe - the prospective lieutenant functioned as a *Kettenfuhrer,* or squadron leader. His personal preference led him to opt for a fighter pilot's career.

In March 1935, the fighter school was officially activated. Galland was transferred to the 1st Fighter Wing in Doberitz near Berlin. Due to the rapid growth of the Luftwaffe, he was soon transferred from the 1st group to the newly-formed II group in Juterbog-Damm. During advanced aerobatic training, he crashed and was seriously injured.

Through a number of tricks he managed not to be grounded and soon was transferred to III group in Bernburg. While test flying a He-51, he suffered another accident. Hunting License No. 317 was issued about that time, from which grew his second major passion; hunting.

Inländer-Jahresjagdschein

Gültig im ganzen Reich * Nr. 317

für den Leutnant Adolf Galland geb. am 19.3.12

wohnhaft zu Bernburg / Saale

Jagdkreis Westhavelland

gültig vom 24.8. 1936 bis 31.3. 1937

Rathenow den 24 Aug 1936

Der Landrat.

i.V.

A. Galland

(Unterschrift des Inhabers)

Für diesen Jagdschein ist eine Gebühr von 50 RM. entrichtet.
Inhaber ist Mitglied des Reichsbundes „Deutsche Jägerschaft".

With the Condor Legion in the Spanish Civil War

On 8 May 1937, Galland arrived at the Spanish harbor of El Ferrol with the title of "tourist group director." In the beginning, he was responsible for leading a headquarters company, but six months later he took command of 3/J88, the Mickey Mouse Squadron. By that time the First and Second Squadrons had converted to the Bf-109 (ME-109). Galland and his squadron, however, continued flying the obsolescent He-51, which was operated primarily in the close air support role. The experience he accumulated during this period became of great advantage to him in the early years of the Second World War.

The headquarters was based at an old convent in Avila. During their off-duty time, the officers drove 60 kilometers (37 miles) into the mountains to the *Parador de Gredos* hotel. There, the war was temporarily forgotten on hunting trips, especially when tracking the rare ibex.

The *Cabra Hispanica* hunting trophy from the Gredos-mountain range.
This trophy can be seen today in Galland's home.

The marginally-prepared Spanish airfields were the cause of a great many accidents. Nose-overs and ground loops were often the end of a well-meant takeoff or landing, as the wreckage in the background indicates. However, the Spanish pilots had even less luck with their aircraft.

The Mickey Mouse squadron symbol of 3/J88 is recognizable next to the white cross indicating the commander's He-51. At that period the Mouse had not yet added the typical Galland cigar and battle-axe.

Galland took a fancy to thick Brazilian cigars in Spain, and they became a permanent part of his profile. It was at that time that a close friendship began between "Lieutenant Neumann" and the "Captain" which continues to this day.

Major Gotthard Handrick, group commander of J88, third from the left, visits the Third Squadron after a chilly night, enjoying the warm sunshine.

Captain Galland and Lieutenant Ehle waiting for operations to begin. Walter Ehle, one of the pioneers of the German night fighters, was killed in a landing crash on 17 November 1943. At that time he had 36 victories.

Scramble: A scramble for a low-level attack on enemy trenches. Because of the heavy dust, the squadron took off in a wide front. The captain's aircraft in the foreground.

In April 1938, Lieutenant Werner Molders took over the Third Squadron at La Cenia. After several extensions Galland was finally returned to Germany. Molders assumed command on 24 May 1938. The squadron continued flying close support missions until July when it re-equipped with Bf 109s. The old He-51s were assigned to the newly-organized Fourth Squadron of J88.

The departure time has come. The men say goodbye to their "old captain" in front of the Ju-52 which took Galland back to Germany.

Im Namen
des
Deutſchen Volkes
verleihe ich
dem Oberleutnant
Adolf Galland
in Anerkennung
ſeiner ganz hervorragenden Leiſtungen
als Freiwilliger im ſpaniſchen Freiheitskampf
das
Deutſche Spanien-Kreuz
in
Gold mit Schwertern und Brillanten
Berlin, den 6. Juni 1939
Der Führer
und
Oberſte Befehlshaber
der Wehrmacht

AG was awarded the Spanish Cross in Gold with Diamonds for his achievements in developing and perfecting close air support missions. Only nine from the Congor Legion were awarded this high decoration; only two of them were alive in 1983.

Flying the Henschel 123 in Poland

After his return from Spain - and a short vacation - First Lieutenant Galland got a new job in the Air Ministry in Berlin. The experience gained in Spain was to be exploited. In the shortest possible time, two close air support wings had to be set up. After a few weeks, five groups were ready for operations. All of Galland's efforts for transfer to fighters remained temporarily unsuccessful. As captain of the Forth Squadron in the II Group of Instruction Wing 2, he participated in the Polish campaign.

The Fourth Squadron, led by Lieutenant Galland, was equipped with the Henschel Hs-123. The 123 was a robust and effective workhorse. The planes of Galland's squadron carried the Mickey Mouse insignia, but now in a different version. In addition to a cigar, Mickey now carries a pistol and a battle-axe. Later on this same insignia was painted on his fighter aircraft.

A brief moment of relaxation on an airfield in Poland.

The "123" is prepared for a mission. In the foreground are crates containing 100-lb. bombs.

The Fourth Squadron approaching a concentration of enemy troops. Under the short lower wing, the bombs are clearly seen. The letters "L-2" (below the cockpit) identify this aircraft as belonging to *Lehrgeschwader* 2.

Despite 75 missions in 18 days (over 4 combat sorties per day), Galland still found time for his hobby - hunting. Soon the soldiers were complaining, "we can't take it any longer - every day we eat nothing but pheasant". A very understandable comment, judging by this photograph.

Sadness shows in the mens' faces. Major Spielvogel, group commander, has crashed in the Warsaw area. During the 18-day campaign, the group lost 10 pilots. The unit was transferred to Braunschweig to recuperate. On 1 October 1939, First Lieutenant Galland was promoted to captain.

When the weather was nice, the office work was done out doors. First Lieutenant Galland standing in the middle, Lieutenant Panten to the left.

Fighter Pilot Against France and England

Captain Galland's efforts to get transferred to fighters were finally successful. His first assignment was operations officer of Fighter Wing 27 in Krefeld, and later in Monchengladbach. For three weeks he represented the three group commanders during their vacations. For Galland, the first months in the West were filled with paperwork. Then, as the blitz started on 10 May 1940, Galland could not be kept on the ground. Between 12 May and 9 June 1940, he gained 12 aerial victories.

A JG-27 flight on a fighter sweep. The open "finger four" formation developed in Spain remained the standard of German fighters on all the fronts. Much later, the British also adopted this formation.

On 10 June 1940, Captain Galland was transferred to JG-26 and took command of its III Group. Before the end of the French campaign, AG claimed three further victories on June 14th. The photo shows Galland in an Me-109 with the "flying dog" group insignia.

Mission briefing with the squadron leaders of III Group. The lifejackets indicate a mission over water. Galland won the respect and admiration of the group very quickly, not only because of his earlier victories but also those gained within III/JG-26.

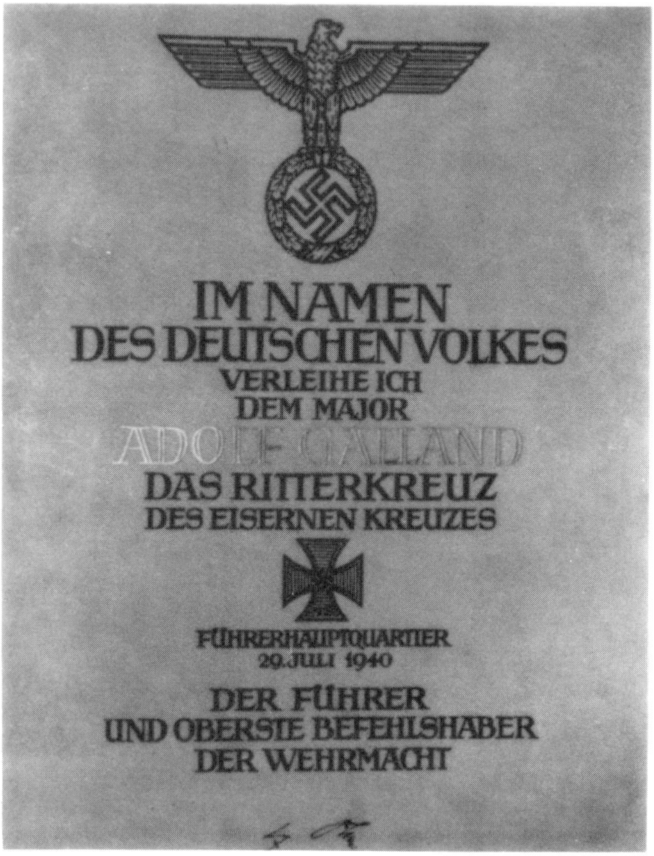

IM NAMEN
DES DEUTSCHEN VOLKES
VERLEIHE ICH
DEM MAJOR
ADOLF GALLAND
DAS RITTERKREUZ
DES EISERNEN KREUZES

FÜHRERHAUPTQUARTIER
29. JULI 1940

DER FÜHRER
UND OBERSTE BEFEHLSHABER
DER WEHRMACHT

After promotion to major on 18 July 1940, Galland was awarded the Knight's Cross to the Iron Cross on 1 August. This was a result of 17 victories and countless low-level missions during the campaign.

The well-known Luftwaffe magazine *Der Adler* congratulates the newly decorated officers.

Wie sie das Ritterkreuz erwarben

Major Hitschhold

Major Graf Schönborn

Major Galland

Oberstleutnant von Bülow

Oberstleutnant von Bülow, der schon im Weltkrieg als junger Jagdflieger sechs Gegner besiegte, ist seit April Kommodore des Jagdgeschwaders Richthofen, das unter seiner Führung stolze Erfolge erringen konnte. Es hat wesentlichen Anteil an der Vernichtung der feindlichen Luftwaffe. Im Verlauf der großen Luftschlacht über Portland, am 11. August dieses Jahres, schoß das Geschwader unter Führung seines Kommodore 22 feindliche Flugzeuge ab. Damit erreichte es die stolze Zahl von 242 Abschüssen in der Luft und 40 Zerstörungen am Boden.

Major Hitschhold hat als Staffelführer einer Stukastaffel in Polen und als Kommandeur einer Stukagruppe im Westen außerordentlichen Schneid und größte Einsatzbereitschaft bewiesen und seinem Verband in der Luft zu kriegsentscheidenden Erfolgen geführt. Ruhmesdaten seiner Stukagruppe sind: Fort Eben Emael, die Forts Pontisse und Flamelle, Tirlemont und Loewen. Im Raume von Gembleux konnte die Sturzkampfgruppe zum Durchbruch durch die Dyle-Stellung beitragen. Bei Boulogne, Calais, Dünkirchen und Gravelines konnte die Einschiffung geschlagener englischer Truppen verhindert werden. Insgesamt hat die Gruppe 164000 Tonnen Schiffsraum versenkt oder schwer beschädigt. Weiter zeichnete sich die Gruppe beim Übergang über die Aisne, bei den Kämpfen an Marne und Seine aus.

Major Graf Schönborn führte schon in Polen als Gruppenkommandeur seine Stukagruppe mit bestem Erfolg. Im Westen erwarb sich seine Gruppe Ruhm bei Maastricht, Antwerpen, Tirlemont und Loewen. Sie hat ferner hervorragenden Anteil an den Erfolgen der Stukaangriffe auf die Festungswerke von Lüttich und Namur sowie an dem Einbruch in die Maginotlinie bei Sedan. Als Geschwaderkommodore führte Major Graf Schönborn sein Geschwader mit beispiellosem Schneid in den Einsätzen gegen die Dyle-Stellung, in den Angriffen auf Boulogne, Calais und Dünkirchen. Hier vernichtete das Geschwader zwei große Transporter und einen Zerstörer. Weitere Einsätze erfolgten bei St. Quentin, beim Durchbruch durch die Aisne-Stellung und anderen Schlachtorten.

Major Galland zeichnete sich als Gruppenkommandeur eines Jagdgeschwaders durch ganz besonderes Draufgängertum aus. Bis zur Auszeichnung mit dem Ritterkreuz brachte er 14 Gegner im Luftkampf zum Absturz. Major Galland, der als erfolgreichster Tiefangriffs-Flieger gilt, hat mit seiner Gruppe viele erfolgreiche Tiefangriffe durchgeführt. Dabei gelang es, am 19. Juni drei Flakbatterien zu vernichten.

Hauptmann Desau hat sich als Jagdflieger besonders ausgezeichnet. Bei der Verleihung des Ritterkreuzes hatte er 20 feindliche Flugzeuge abgeschossen. Seine stete Einsatzbereitschaft und sein tapferes Verhalten sind vorbildlich.

Oberfeldwebel Renz nahm mit seinem Geschwader an den Einsätzen gegen England, Norwegen und im Westen erfolgreich teil.

A scene which often repeats itself: after a successful combat mission, Galland returns to Audembert, the fighter wing base. After landing, he is enthusiastically welcomed by his mechanics and fellow officers.

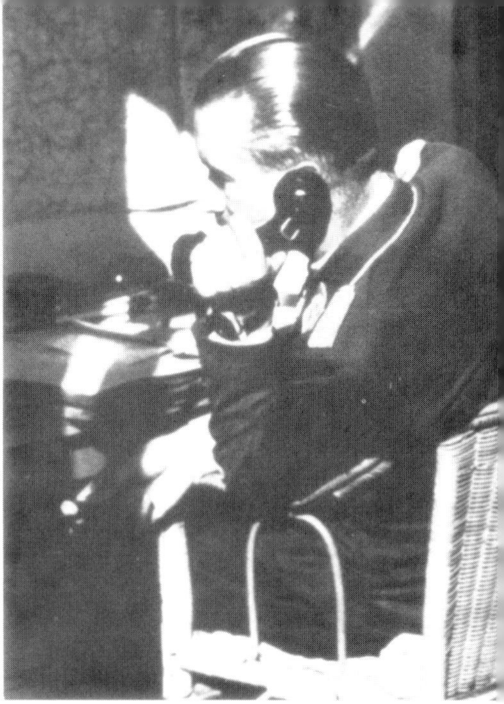

On 22 August 1940 the young Major Galland became *Kommodore* of Fighter Wing 26. Now he was responsible for the planning and operations of the three groups in his wing. The former *Kommodore,* Major General Ritter von Schleich, who earned the *Pour le Merite* as a World War I fighter pilot, maintained contact with his former wing and its new commander.

Recently promoted to Reichsmarshal, Herman Goering visits his fighter wings on the Channel. The young Kommodores of JG-51, Major Werner Molders, and JG-26, Major Adolf Galland, brief him on their successes and disappointments. In the photo, left, next to Goering, is General Loerzer. Behind Molders is General Kastner, Chief of Luftwaffe Personnel.

During the Western Campaign and in the beginning of the Battle of Britain, the Hurricane was the fighter aircraft most frequently encountered. It was slightly inferior to the Me-109 in top speed and rate of climb. However, in the hands of an experienced pilot it was capable of extremely successful combat.

The Spitfire - an outstanding and elegant aircraft - was more or less equal to the German fighters as regards speed. However, it was more maneuverable and had excellent rate of climb. In certain conditions, the German fighter pilots would have exchanged their Messerschmitts for Spitfires.

During the Battle of Britain, the German fighters had a difficult job in adequately protecting their bombers. Since drop tanks to extend the range were not yet available, the pilots often had to break away in the middle of combat to return to their fields on the opposite side of the channel before running out of fuel. In the photo an attacking Spitfire can be seen at the moment it has been hit and starts to go down in flames.

Major Galland returns to his airfield, rocking his wings during a low-level pass to indicate a victory. His crew chief, Corporal Meyer, is standing on the wing, the first one to congratulate him.

The major's face still reflects the intensity and strain of the recent air battle.

In front of the Me-109, a glass of champagne celebrates the victory; then a quick debriefing with First Lieutenant Kienzle. The latter was subsequently shot down over London and so seriously wounded that a leg had to be amputated.

Late August at Caffiers: First Lieutenant Schopfel (third on left) Commander of III Group, discusses a rendezvous point with the bomber formations with the Kommodore and First Lieutenant Muncheberg, captain of the Seventh Squadron. The group Surgeon, Dr. Rosenkranz, stands behind them adding his comments.

Sergeant Harmann paints the commander's personal insignia, the Mickey Mouse, on his new Me-109. He will now fly the "Emil" with the number "red one."

In Audembert Galland describes a tricky moment. His reliable wingman, Master Sergeant Hegenauer (right) and Captain Pingel (second on right) and Dr. Rosenkranz listen carefully.

Once again, Reichsmarshal Goring visits the fighter groups on the channel coast. From Cap Gris Nez — the nearest place to England — he watches the wings flying into combat against the British. In the photo from the left; General Grauert, General Bodenschatz, Goring, Field Marshal Kesselring, Colonel Schmidt as well as Generals Loerzer and Lohr.

The Reichsmarshal meets wing-commanders Molders and Galland in front of his private train. During the discussion, Goring asked their opinion of whether they should shoot at British pilots who have bailed out. Both officers immediately rejected the suggestion. After a moment of silence, Goring assured them that he and his fellow pilots in WW I would have reacted the same way. When asked what he could do to strengthen the fighters' ability to escort German bombers, Molders asked for higher-powered engines for his Messerschmitts. Sarcastically, Galland replied, "Please re-equip my wing with Spitfires, Herr Reichsmarshal!"

After that meeting, lengthy discussions continued at Audembert. The subject can easily be guessed.

Caffiers Airfield - Pas de Calis. Captain Gerhard Schopfel, commander of JG-26's III Group, is awarded the Knight's Cross for 20 aerial victories on 11 September 1940. Among the well-wishers are Lt. Col. Vieck (left) and Lieutenant Haibock (right).

Captain Pingel, commander of I Group JG-26, and other officers during a hunt. Rolf Pingel was awarded the Knight's Cross on 14 September 1940 after his 15th victory. After his 26th victory, he was shot down on 10 July 1941 near Dover and became a prisoner of war.

During a pause in a hunt, Galland sits on a ploughshear. The result could be labeled "light field artillery."

September 1940. The Kommodore has shot down a Hurricane north of Rochester near the mouth of the Thames River. It is victory number 40. Corporal Meyer smiles while the technical staff congratulates the commander. In the photo, starting from left: Captain Cousin, (with the champagne bottle), First Lieutenant Rotenberg (Galland's adjutant), Corporal Meyer, war-correspondent, and Major Galland.

A maintenance man keeps score.

The VIP visitors at Le Touquet. General Udet and General Milch (right) in a discussion with Major Galland. On the left General von Doring,

Galland was the third officer in the German Armed Forces to be awarded the Oak Leaves to the Knight's Cross, which occurred on 25 September 1940. After receiving Major Werner Molders and the General of Mountain Troops, Dietl, Adolf Hitler personally congratulated the Kommodore of JG-26 in the new chancellory in Berlin. In a private discussion, Galland reported his successes, but he also reported on the problems facing his pilots over the Channel.

In front of the Brandenburg Gate, another photograph was taken as a reminder of this day.

This photograph, though often published, has a place in this book. Galland loves dogs and continues to the present date. His hunting setter, Schweinebauch, received two Dachshounds as company.

The faithful setter even was a frequent passenger on inspection flights in the Fieseler Storch.

Italian fighter pilots visit their German comrades on the Channel. They admire the Kommodore's rudder which now shows 45 victories. Number 45 was on 15 October 1940 south of Rochester. The British pilot was able to parachute to safety from his crippled aircraft. Next to Major Molders, Galland was now the second highest-scoring German fighter pilot.

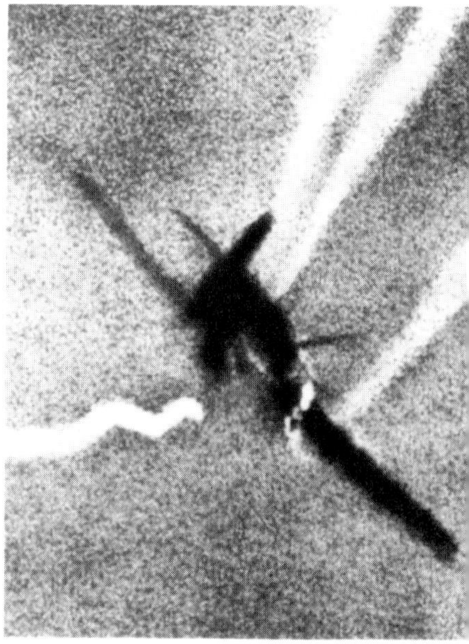

On 1 November 1940, JG-26 reported the *Kommodore's* 50th aerial victory. This milestone is scored by shooting a Spitfire out of a large group of machines. The press reported on this victory in great detail.

VÖLKISCHER BEOBACHTER

Die Seite des Soldaten

Major Gallands 50. Luftsieg

Von Kriegsberichter Hans Jütte

dnb. PK., 5. November

Ein Ehrentag für das Jagdgeschwader! Waffeind kommen mehrere Maschinen von den Einsätzen gegen England auf den Feldflugplatz in Nordfrankreich zurück. Der Kommodore selbst schießt an diesem Tage im Luftkampf drei englische Jäger ab und erreicht damit seinen 47., 48. und 49. Luftsieg. Groß ist die Freude beim Geschwader. Nicht allein wegen des großen Gesamterfolges, sondern auch deswegen, weil der Kommodore unmittelbar vor dem Abschuß steht, der das halbe Hundert rundet.

31. Oktober. Regenböen trommeln an die Fenster und peitschen über den Platz. In den Lüften donnern die Motoren der benachbarten Fliegerverbände. Dem Jagdgeschwader bringt der letzte Oktobertag wohlverdiente Ruhe.

1. November. Der Sturm hat sich im Laufe der Nacht gelegt. Strahlender Sonnenschein vertreibt die letzten Wolken — ein ideales Herbstwetter. Alle im Geschwader fühlen es, als die Maschinen mit dem Kommodore an der Spitze in der Mittagsstunde starten: Heute ist der fünfzigste fällig!

„Jagdschutz für leichte Kampfflieger", so lautet der Auftrag, den das Geschwader erhalten hat. Unangefochten erreichen die Verbände das Ziel. Unter dem Schutz der Jäger können sie ihre Bomben über London abladen und auch noch den Erfolg beobachten. Dann heißt es: Kurs heimwärts. Der Kommodore löst sich mit seinem Rottenführer vom Verband und befiehlt für das gesamte Geschwader freie Jagd.

Irgendwo im Luftraum hat er einzelne Punkte gesichtet. Bald zeigt sich, daß hier ein Pulk Spitfires dahinbraust. Genau ist nicht auszumachen, wie viel Maschinen es sind. Aber so 16 oder 18 mögen es doch sein. Eine stattliche Übermacht! Die Angriffsposition ist aber günstig. Noch haben die Engländer die sich heranpirschenden deutschen Jäger nicht bemerkt.

Mit Bedacht sucht sich Major Galland „seine Spitfire" heraus. Jetzt ist es so weit! Aus nächster Nähe eröffnet der Kommodore das Feuer, und unter den Garben seiner Bordwaffen splittern einzelne Teile der englischen Jagdmaschine ab.

Ein neuer Feuerstoß auf die Spitfire, die in diesem Augenblick aufgehört hat, ein Flugzeug zu sein. Sie platzt buchstäblich auseinander und flattert in Einzelstücken in die Tiefe.

Fast im gleichen Augenblick kommt der Rottenführer in ähnlicher Lage zum Schuß, und der zweite Engländer ist erledigt. Ehe aber die beiden deutschen Jäger sich ein neues Opfer suchen können, gehen die Engländer stiften ... Sie versuchen es gar nicht, sich in einen Kampf mit den zwei Me's einzulassen.

Mit Jubel wird Major Galland bei seiner Landung begrüßt. Als er eine Stunde später erneut gegen England startet, zieren fünfzig Striche das Leitwerk der Maschine!

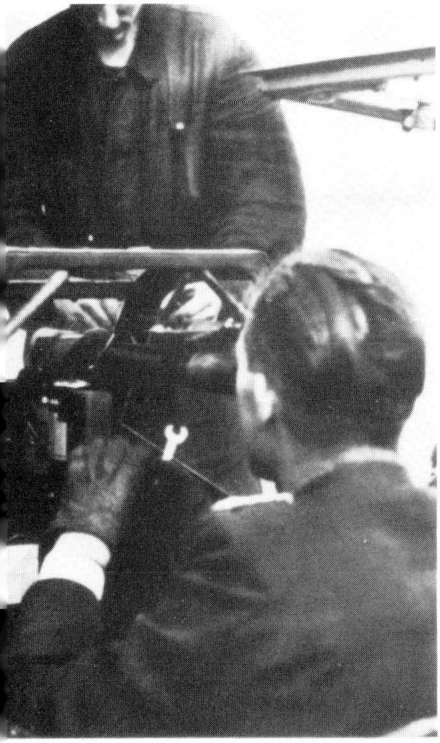

Galland's Messerschmitt was equipped with an experimental telescope sight. His armorer, Corporal Olemotz, had finished the installation in these photos, but the *Kommodore* made the final adjustments. After being tested on several missions the sight was found to be useless.

On 1 November 1940, after a brief four months as major, Galland was promoted to lieutenant colonel. He continued his combat flying.

The recipients of the highest German decorations were immortalized by famous German artists making formal portraits in oil. Here, Galland tried to help the artist with some finishing touches.

Despite having the highest confidence in his mechanics, the "Chief" personally monitors the change of a propeller on his aircraft.

Galland just before a test flight. Corporal Meyer helps with the preflight preparations.

A visit to JG-51. Werner Molders greets a guest, who is still sitting in his aircraft. During the Battle of Britain, both their names are mentioned almost daily in the armed forces communiques. Despite the additional administrative workload resulting from their promotions, both continued to schedule themselves on daily combat missions.

Following a rapid increase in the loss of German aircraft - especially the bombers - daylight attacks against England were terminated. The bombers then operated only at night. The fighter wings were ordered to each convert a squadron of each group into fighter-bombers in order to continue daylight attacks on British targets. These "pin prick tactics" brought no results, while the losses of both fighter-bombers and escorts steadily mounted. The final result of this controversial decision was actually a significant increase in the loss of men and material.

Shortly before Christmas of 1940, Adolf Hitler visited JG-26 on the English Channel. While drinking tea and eating cake in a festive atmosphere of candlelight and open fireplaces, Hitler spoke about the war as "already won," and his unique talent in avoiding a war on two fronts. Even today - after 45 years - it would be difficult to fully describe the inner reaction of the fighter pilots. In the above photo from right to left; Captain Schopfel, Lieutenant Colonel Galland, Hitler, Captain Pingel, Captain Adolph, First Lieutenant Sprick, and directly in front and in the foreground, First Lieutenant Muncheberg.

During the winter of 1940 - 1941, the pilots of the fighter wings stationed on the Channel were given brief leaves. Followed by JG-51, the pilots of JG-26 spent their holidays at Zurs, a beautiful skiing area in the Vorarlberg Mountains. For Galland this would be his first and only holiday during the whole war.

Following a much-needed rest, the wings were brought up to strength and then returned to the Channel coast to resume operations. Galland is photographed by a wing man during a mission.

. . . and landing at Wissant after completing the mission.

The cockpit hatch is opened; instead of fresh air, a cigar is lit.

The then *Jafu 2,* Major General Theo Osterkamp (Uncle Theo), invited several wing *Kommodores* to LeTouquet for his birthday party on 15 April 1941. Lieutenant Colonel Galland takes off from Brest with a basket filled with fresh lobsters and oysters. Making a "little detour" over Kent, he succeeds in attracting the attention of Spitfires, shoots down two of them and continues on his way to the birthday party.

A lively discussion after lunch. In the photo, fro right to left: Major General Osterkamp, Lieutenant Colonel Molders, Galland, Major Dr. Wenzel, aide to Molders, and in the foreground, Major Lutzow.

Field Marshal Milch, Goring's deputy, visits JG-26 during an inspection trip. The *Kommodore* welcomes the guest at his Do-215 transport. Captain Adolph, Commander of III group of JG-26, is being introduced. Adolph had been awarded the Knight's Cross on 13 November 1940 following his 15th aerial victory. He was listed missing in action on 18 September 1941.

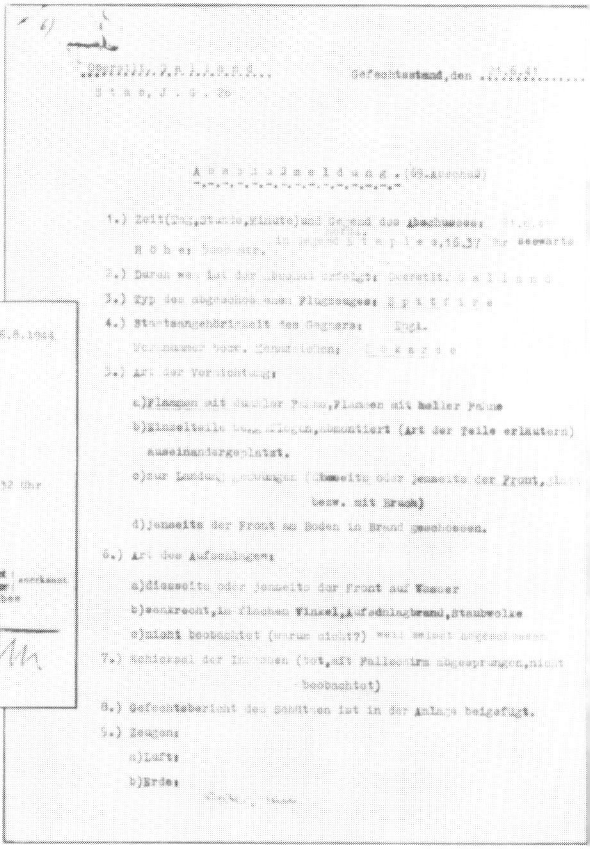

Gefechtsstand, den 21.6.41

Stab, J.G. 26

Abschußmeldung.

1.) Zeit (Tag, Stunde, Minute) und Gegend des Abschusses:
Höhe:
2.) Durch wen ist der Abschuß erfolgt: Oberstlt. Galland
3.) Typ des abgeschossenen Flugzeuges: Spitfire
4.) Staatsangehörigkeit des Gegners: Engl.
5.) Art der Vernichtung:
a) Flammen mit dunkler Fahne, Flammen mit heller Fahne
b) Einzelteile weggeflogen, abmontiert (Art der Teile erläutern) auseinandergeplatzt.
c) zur Landung gezwungen (diesseits oder jenseits der Front, glatt bzw. mit Bruch)
d) jenseits der Front am Boden in Brand geschossen.
6.) Art des Aufschlages:
a) diesseits oder jenseits der Front auf Wasser
b) senkrecht, im flachen Winkel, Aufschlagbrand, Staubwolke
c) nicht beobachtet (warum nicht?)
7.) Schicksal der Insassen (tot, mit Fallschirm abgesprungen, nicht beobachtet)
8.) Gefechtsbericht des Schützen ist in der Anlage beigefügt.
9.) Zeugen:
a) Luft:
b) Erde:

Der Reichsminister der Luftfahrt
und Oberbefehlshaber der Luftwaffe
Chef f.Ausz.u.Diszpl.(V)
Az. 29 Nr. 429/44

Berlin, den 16.8.1944

An Stab/J.G.26

Dem Stab/J.G.26
wird der Abschuß eines britischen Kampfflugzeuges vom Typ
Bristol "Blenheim" am 21.6.1941, 12.32 Uhr
durch Obstlt. Galland

als sechsundachtzigster (86.)

Luftsieg des Stabes anerkannt.

I.A.

21 June 1941 - despite three victories obtained this date, it would be a "black day" in Galland's memories. About noon, a Blenheim bomber formation, escorted by about 50 British fighters, was spotted. Diving from a higher altitude, Galland shot down two bombers. His aircraft was seriously damaged by the escorting Spitfires and he made a belly landing. In the late afternoon of the same day - now flying his second 109, he had a second meeting with roving Spitfires. His 70th victory went down in flames. Galland's machine was seriously damaged and he was hit by shrapnel in the head and right arm, and the Me-109 started to burn. Despite his injuries, using the last bit of his strength, Galland managed to pen the canopy and bail out. Rushed to the German Navy Hospital at Hardinghem, his injuries were treated by a navy surgeon and friend, Dr. Heim. Galland was allowed to smoke his cigar on the operating table! Early that evening he left the hospital and returned

to his wing, where he learned from General Osterkamp that he had been awarded the Swords to the Oak Leaves of the Knight's Cross. Galland thus became the first German soldier to receive this decoration. With the award came a strict order to avoid combat missions.

A few days later Galland resumed flying and tested his two brand-new 109s. One was equipped with additional armor plate, designed by Corporal Meyer to protect the back of the pilot's head. Galland criticized the installation since he bumped his head repeatedly on 2 July. However, it saved his life the same day during a "test flight." JG-26 attacked a formation of RAF bombers escorted by fighters. A 20mm shell exploded against the new armor plate and, again wounded, Galland managed a safe landing. Ordered to Hitler's headquarters in the *Wolfschanze* at Rastenburg, he was awarded the Swords. Hitler asked him to "be more prudent during aerial combat," but there was no mention of the earlier grounding order. The photo shows the mangled remains of Galland's Me-109 crash of 21 June 1941.

One of Galland's close friends was Major Wolfgang Schellman. Credited with 12 victories in Spain, he received the Spanish Cross in Gold with Diamonds. After 12, twelve victories during the Battle of Britain he became wing commander of JG-2 *Richthofen.* The following year he was named *Kommodore* of JG-27, which fought on the Russian Front. On 22 June 1941 he shot down a Rata so closely that fragments of his victim forced him to bail out. "Gedalie" Schellmann, the victor of 26 combats, was killed on the ground.

OBERSTLEUTNANT GALLAND

OBERSTLEUTNANT MÖLDERS

An der Luftschlacht des 21. Juni 1941 hat Oberstleutnant Galland durch hervorragende Führung seines Geschwaders und durch Abschuß von drei Gegnern besonderen Anteil gehabt. Oberstleutnant Mölders schoß am Tage darauf seinen 72. Gegner in der Luft ab. Der Führer hat aus Anlaß dieses heldenhaften Einsatzes beiden Offizieren das von ihm neugestiftete Eichenlaub mit Schwertern zum Ritterkreuz des Eisernen Kreuzes verliehen und ihnen ein entsprechendes Glückwunschtelegramm gesandt

The official Luftwaffe magazine, *Adler,* reported the award of the Swords to Lieutenant Colonel Galland. One day later Werner Molders, *Kommodore* of JG-51, also received this highest decoration.

Operational headquarters at Audembert. The *Kommodore* of JG-2, Major Walter Oesau, visits Galland. Oesau is the third commodore to be awarded the swords, on 15 July 1941. From left to right, Captain Schopfel, Galland, Colonel Huth and Major Oesau.

Another guest at Audembert was General Oshima, the Japanese Ambassador to Germany. The general was noted for being able to drink enormous quantities of hard liquor while staying perfectly sober.

Galland flies his beloved Me-108 *Taifun* on a visit to JG-51. Colonel Molders and his wing are being transferred to the eastern border of Germany. It is just before the attack on Russia.

This cartoon was drawn by General Udet during the height of the Battle of Britain, showing the two well-known fighter aces as rivals with their victories. Udet was known not only as an outstanding pilot, but a very talented artist as well.

Before takeoff, the Kommodore chatting with Captain Schmid. The capable leader of the Eighth Squadron, awarded the Knight's Cross after his 25th victory, vanished without a trace during a mission on 6 November 1941.

Over-water missions required special emergency equipment for the pilots. Included were life jackets, compressed air bottles, flare pistols and smoke signals as well as a dye marker. A small inflatable one-man rubber dinghy was stowed in the cockpit. In this picture; from left to right; Lieutenant Richter, Lieutenant Colonel Galland and Captain Schmid. Richter, after scoring three victories, was shot down on 7 November 1941.

The photos on this page document the increasing savagery of the air battles. The *Kommodore* climbs from his Me-109 in a state of exhaustion. His face shows the extraordinary tension and concentration of the last hours. His British opponent was a very capable adversary who damaged the Me-109 rather badly before he was put out of action. Galland's engine was hit several times and an oil line had been shot away.

9 August 1941: heavy air combat over the Pas de Calais. Galland downed two Spitfires from a formation. Another staff officer claimed a third aircraft. An RAF pilot was seen bailing out: Wing Comander Douglas Bader. Bader, a brilliant combat pilot with two artificial legs, struggled from his impacted Spitfire, leaving one of his artificial limbs jammed in the machine. Injured while landing his parachute, Bader was rushed to the military hospital at St. Omer. His first request was salvage of the artificial leg from the wreckage of his Spitfire. It was recovered and immediately repaired by the mechanics of JG-26.

When Galland learned the prisoner was capable of walking on the repaired limb, he asked to have Bader brought to his headquarters at Audembert. Bader seemed to appreciate the welcome he received.

The JG26 group commanders also were invited to join Bader and Galland for afternoon tea. Afterwards, the commander invited his guest for a tour of the airfield installations. Bader, becoming more at ease, asked to have a message transmitted to England . . . "He (Bader) is feeling well and asks for his spare set of artificial legs, a new uniform and pipe and tobacco". Galland promised to do everthing possible to fulfill his guest's unusual request. Bader especially was interested in the Me-109 which was giving him and his RAF comrades so much trouble. He was invited to climb into Galland's aircraft, where Galland answered Bader's many questions. However, Galland was forced to refuse Bader's request to be allowed a short test hop in Galland's Me-109. That same evening, after a cordial farewell, Bader was returned to the St. Omer hospital.

Galland immediately contacted Goring in order to forward Bader's request. Communication was established with the RAF via the international rescue frequency, and receipt of the message was confirmed. This action became proof that chivalry and humanity had not completely disappeared between these two air forces. Shortly afterwards, the airfields of JG-26 on the Channel coast were bombed by the RAF; immediately following the attack a message confirmed that, in addition to the bombs, a container with Bader's articles had also been "delivered." (Smaller picture at bottom of page).

After the end of the war, the two met again when Galland was a prisoner in England. On that occasion, the famous British pilot presented Galland with a box of excellent cigars. This was the beginning of a life-long friendship between the two.

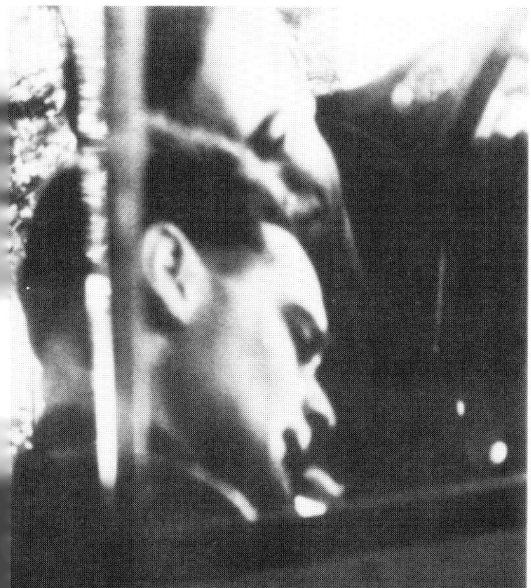

Frequently Galland was ordered to *Reichmarshall* Goring's Headquarters in East Prussia to brief him. For Galland, these trips to East Prussia, often ending with a hunt, became unforgettable highlights. The photo shows him with the *Reichmarshall's* game wardens in Elchwald, East Prussia, where Galland has just taken a trophy.

Captain Muncheberg was reassigned from the Mediterranean to the Channel front to take over the command of the third group. He had just been awarded the Oak Leaves to his Knight's Cross; a good excuse for Galland to organize a pheasant hunt. This group included Colonel Huth, Captain Muncheberg, Galland and the leader of JG-27, Count Ergo von Kageneck, who was fatally wounded during an air battle over the Mediterranean on 12 January 1942.

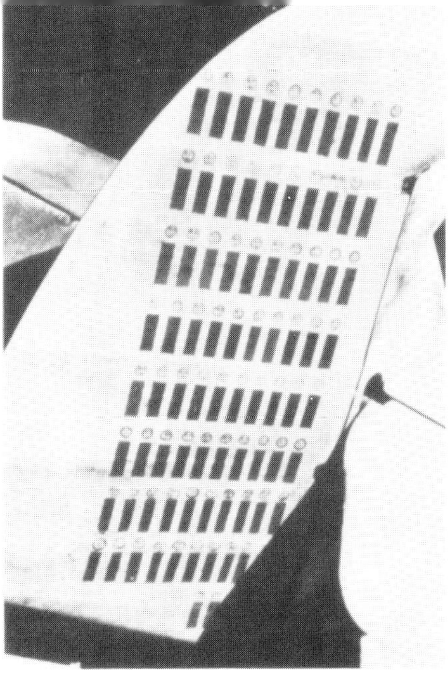

The rudder of Galland's plane records his 84th victory. Lieutenant Colonel Vieck (left) and Captain Ewald - both friends of Galland - congratulate the *Kommodore* on his latest aerial victory.

In mid-1941 a new fighter type was delivered to the front. The Second Group of JG-26 was the first to be re-equipped with the Focke-Wulf FW-190. On 1 September the conversion was completed. The FW-190 would shortly become a highly respected adversary among the British pilots.

Galland's two younger brothers - Wilhelm-Ferdinand and Paul - were also flying in JG-26 at this time.

Galland's plan, proposed in January of 1943, to have JG-26 exchange places with JG-54, which was then operational on the Eastern front, was soon abandoned. The operational conditions in these two theaters of war were too diverse to allow the exchange. The First Group of JG-26 operated six months on the Eastern front while the Third Group of JG-54 fought in the West. The following letter was written by Adolf Galland to his brother Wilhelm, preparing him for his new tasks as group commander in the totally different combat conditions in the East.

Dear Wutz: *11 January 1943*

Thank you for your letter which pleased me by the news of your promotion, as well as by your attitude. My congratulations.

To continue our last discussion, here are a few additional comments. It is clear that you will be very closely watched during the beginning of your service as Commander. It is easy to follow a leader who did nothing by simply doing a little bit, but I remind you of my advice to fight like a lion for your group. Everyone, down to the most junior airmen, must be convinced that you are a strong leader who genuinely cares about every single individual; when they feel that, they will go through fire for you. You must be in complete control because new and serious challenges face you. Nothing happens by itself and nothing corrects itself. Every detail must be rehearsed a thousand times and every success has to be earned. You will not believe how much work a man can accomplish. You cannot tolerate any mistake that could have been avoided by better planning, clearer orders or more efficient operation.

You should not be too familiar with your officers. Despite that, you can still be their best friend. Concern and consideration for the junior officers and enlisted men will pay for itself a thousand fold. The most important principle is to insure that those under you feel that their commander understands their worries; that the commander can be approached by anyone in the group; that what he demands of the group is necessary, and that you would never demand of them more than what you are willing to demand of yourself.

Particularly on the Eastern front, this will be of great importance. Individual victories in the air should be subordinate to the overall success of the group. Enough rubs off on the leader in any case. It may well be that, in the East the group's first missions will be independent of and quite far away from the rest of your wing. Especially in this case, careful and detailed preparation is essential. It will all be very new for all of you and all must be completely dedicated to the goals because otherwise it will lead to grim catastrophies.

In conclusion, a few words about your ***Kommodore****. There can be but one attitude on your part - complete loyalty and discipline. Without those factors the rest will be impossible. This is the only attitude you can adopt; there is no alternative. Your* ***Kommodore*** *carries the complete responsibility and can only lead successfully if* *he is able to rely unconditionally on his subordinate commanders. If that is not there, the whole wing will fail. The concept of a parliamentary consensus, with its relatively free and relaxed compromises, does not exist anymore. There is but one decision and that is the* ***Kommodore's*** *and it is valid for the whole wing. I would never tolerate dissent in a wing under my command, one that would not support me in that fashion.*

So now, "Wutz," you know what I and the family expect of you. I am always available for help and advice if you feel you need it. I wish you every success in one of the finest commands an officer can have and I know that you will do it. Hals und Beinbruch!

(Break a leg)

Your Brother Adolf

Wilhelm-Ferdinand, nicknamed "Wutz," transferred from the anti-aircraft branch to fighters with the help of his famous brother. On 23 July 1941, he scored his first victory over the Channel. On 8 May 1943, while commander of the Second Group, he was awarded the Knight's Cross after his 41st victory in the West. He registered 55 aerial victories before being killed in combat near Liege on 17 August 1943.

Paul, the youngest of the Galland brothers, nicknamed "PG," transferred from the signal corps to fighters. After some initial problems, he became a successful fighter pilot. Lieutenant Paul Galland died in combat on 30 October 1942 having achieved 17 victories in his short career.

17 November 1941 was the date of the death of General Ernest Udet. Although radio and press report that he died testing a new aircraft, in reality he committed suicide. He sensed, far in advance of many others, how the war would end. He chose suicide when he began to break down under the load of ever-increasing responsibilities which he was unable to master. Hitler ordered a state funeral. The most highly decorated fighter and bomber pilots formed the honor guard for Udet's coffin as it moved through the streets of Berlin to the Invaliden Cemetery.

A few days later another funeral procession moved through the streets of Berlin. The first General of the Fighter Arm, Werner Molders, was killed in a crash while being flown from the Crimea to Berlin. His death was a great loss, not only for the Fighter Arm, but for all of Germany. His Heinkel III crashed during a bad-weather approach to an airfield near Breslau; the aircraft lost an engine and evidently stalled while trying to overfly a power line. Molders and the flight mechanic were killed in the crash; the pilot died while being transported to the hospital. Only Molders' operations officer survived. Again, Hitler ordered a state funeral. On 28 November the ceremony took place in the Air Ministry Hall of Honor. Lieutenant Colonel Galland once again was among the guard of honor as the carriage moved to the Invaliden Cemetery.

General of the Fighter Arm

On 4 December 1941, Galland was promoted to colonel, and took Molders' place on 6 December. Goring arrived at Audembert near Wissant, France, to participate in Galland's farewell to his wing. Goring showed special interest in the rudder of Galland's Me-109, which now recorded 94 aerial victories. The figure 69 not only represented the aerial victories that won Galland his Swords to the Knight's Cross, but also reminds him of the mission which very nearly cost him his life.

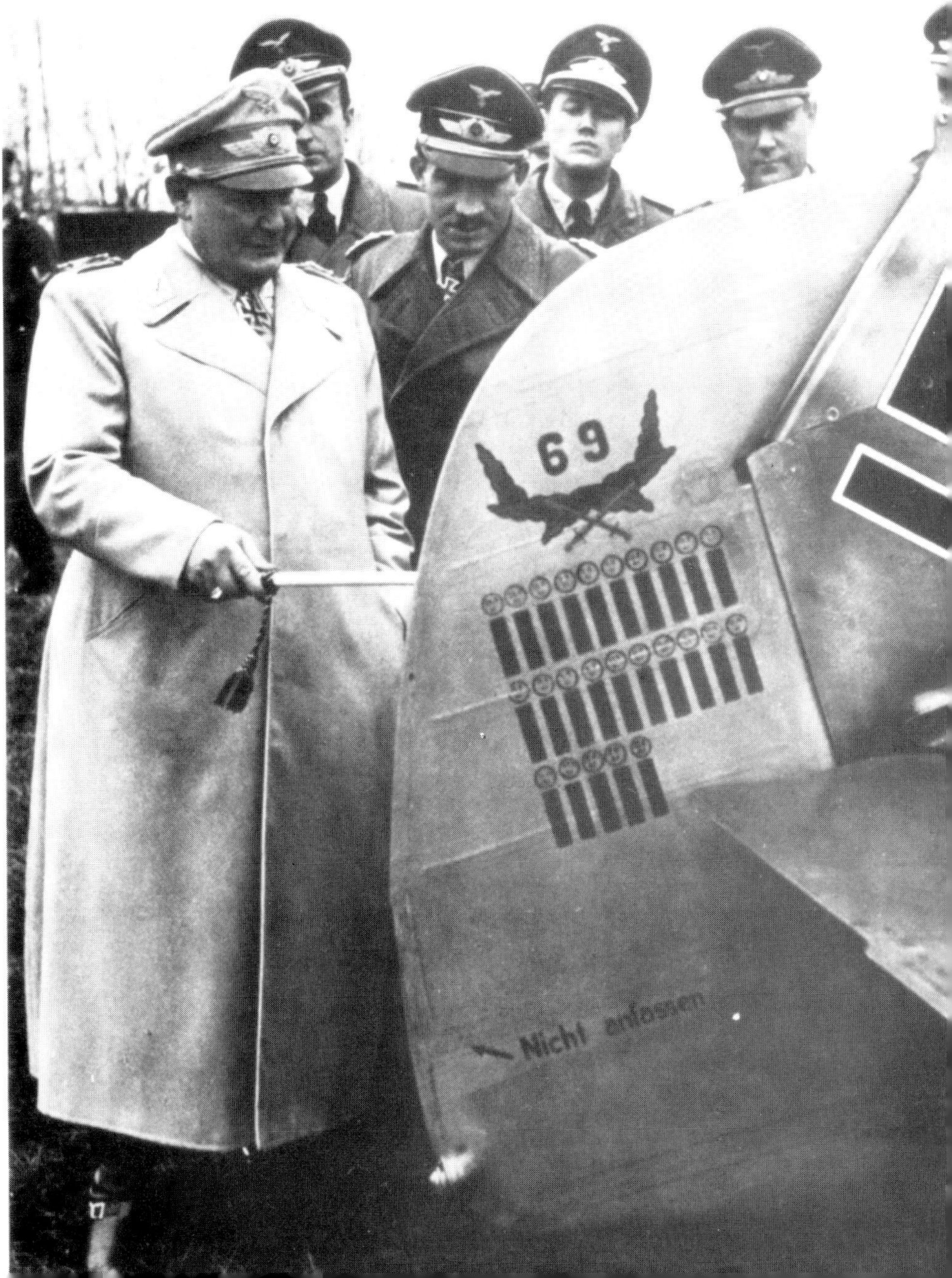

Colonel Galland briefs Goring about the wing-mounted guns and their combat performance.

The Me-109F, always highly polished, seems to be of great interest to Goring.

Major Gerhard Schopfel took over as JG-26 *Kommodore* on 6 December 1941 and remained in that position for over two years, to 10 January 1943.

JG-26 remained on the Western front under Schopfel's command. All three groups were now operating the FW-190 against an increasingly powerful enemy.

The standard on Colonel Galland's staff car. The insignia of the General of the Fighter Arm is divided in a light and dark background, symbolizing the day and night fighter units.

In the special train of the General Staff of the Luftwaffe, code-named "Robinson," a meeting of the Air Staff takes place. Chief of Staff General Jeschonnek, talking to the General of the Fighter Arm, Galland.

Another portrait, but this time with a cigar. Today, this painting is to be seen in Galland's home near Bonn.

In January 1942, the General visited JG-54, the "Green Heart Wing," operating on the northern section of the Eastern front.

The *Kommodore,* Major Hannes Trautloft, received his guest in Rjelbitzy. This airfield, as well as the one at Sieverskaja, had been JG-54's operational base for more than three years.
The group picture (below) in front of headquarters, shows from left to right Dr. Vogel, Major Andres, Major Janke, Major Trautloft, Colonel Galland, Captain Hrabak, Captain Brustellin and First Lieutenant Wende.

In the headquarters "lounge" the scene is more relaxed. Over a glass of champagne, *Kommodore* Trautloft points out some of the more important events recorded in the wing's diary. Left of Galland, Major Andres.

On 28 January 1942, Colonel Galland became the second member of the German Armed Forces ever to receive the Diamonds to the Oak Leaves with Swords to the Knight's Cross. This is at *Wolfsschanze,* Hitler's headquarters near Rastenburg. In the photo starting from the left, Field Marshall General Milch, Field Marshall General Keitel, Colonel Galland, Adolf Hitler and General Jeschonnek.

IM NAMEN
DES DEUTSCHEN VOLKES
VERLEIHE ICH
DEM OBERST
ADOLF GALLAND
DAS EICHENLAUB MIT
SCHWERTERN UND BRILLANTEN
ZUM RITTERKREUZ
DES EISERNEN KREUZES
FÜHRERHAUPTQUARTIER
DEN 28. JANUAR 1942
DER FÜHRER
UND OBERSTE BEFEHLSHABER
DER WEHRMACHT

The "diamonds" were accompanied by this superb hand-crafted certificate in a leather case decorated with gold and diamonds. After the war, the certificate was returned to Galland by an unidentified man who had rescued it from the rubble of Berlin. The leather case disappeared after the war, but the certificate is still in Galland's possession today.

After the award, Goring invited Colonel Galland to a bison hunt in the Schorfheide fields. Galland is visibly proud of this huge trophy.

The "Channel Dash," 11 to 13 February 1942

While protected by a round-the-clock Luftwaffe "shield" for three days and nights, the German Navy succeeded in moving a battle fleet from Brest to Norway. The battleships *Scharnhorst, Gneisenau* and the heavy cruiser *Prinz Eugen* passed through the English Channel under the astonished eyes of the British. As they moved Northeast they were protected by destroyers, torpedo-boats, minesweepers and fast escort ships, while units of day and night fighters formed an aerial umbrella. The fighter defense, supported by the flak from the ships, foiled all the attacks mounted by British torpedo planes and bombers.

A large role in the success of the Channel Dash was played by the young general of the fighters, Adolf Galland.His planning, organization and direction of the participating fighter units allowed complete control of the air over the flotilla. This unique and risky operation was concluded successfully with relatively light losses to the Germans. More than 40 British aircraft were downed by fighters or anti-aircraft fire; the Luftwaffe lost 11 pilots and 17 aircraft.

In late March 1942 the General of the fighters visited JG-51, the *Molders* wing on the eastern front. Lieutenant Colonel Friedrich von Beckh, who replaced Molders as wing commander, is talking to the General. Von Beckh, awarded the Knight's Cross, was listed as missing in action on 21 June 1942.

Captain Hachfeld, nicknamed "Bomber-Willy" because of his leading role in the development of fighter-bomber tactics, introduces one of his most capable pilots. Hachfeld is wearing the fur cap.

In the Spring of 1942, the Luftwaffe High Command met in *Karinhall,* Goring's luxurious country estate on the Schorfheide in the Mecklenburg area. His home often was used for such meetings. In the photograph above, from left to right, the following can be recognized: Field Marshall Milch, Major Teske, General Kastner, Galland, General Lohr, unknown, Field Marshall Sperrle, General Bodenschatz, Goring, unknown, Field Marshall Kesselring, General Stumpf and General Martini.

Once again, General Galland makes an inspection trip. Standing in front of a He-111 he is heartily welcomed by *Jafu 3,* Colonel Max Ibel. To Galland's right is his adjutant and personal friend, 1st Lieutenant Heinrich von Donner.

In the early summer of 1942, the general flew with Captain Schmoller-Haldy in his Siebel Si-104 to Sicily, and from there to North Africa in a Me-110. This trip was to visit JG-27, the desert fighter wing.

The First Group of JG-27 was operational in North Africa in early April of 1941. The II and III Groups, with wing headquarters, followed by year's end. In 1942 this wing carried the main burden of combat in the African theatre. This photograph shows the general accompanied by some of his "desert fighters." On the right, next to Galland is the *Kommodore* of the wing, Lieutenant Colonel Woldenga.

The most successful fighter pilot of the African front was Lieutenant Hans-Joachim Marseille, here seated in his "yellow 13." "Jochen" has just registered his 75th victory and received the Oak Leaf Cluster. He commanded his Me-109 as if it were a musical instrument. His incredible eyesight and outstanding piloting abilities allowed him to attack and down enemy aircraft from almost any tactical position.
The "Star of Africa," as he was nicknamed, was probably the unrivaled virtuoso of WW II's fighter pilots. On 2 September 1942, after his 126th aerial victory, he received the Diamonds to his *Ritterkreuz.* On 30 September 1942, after his 158th aerial victory, he was fatally injured bailing out of his fighter, which had developed a mechanical problem during a routine flight.

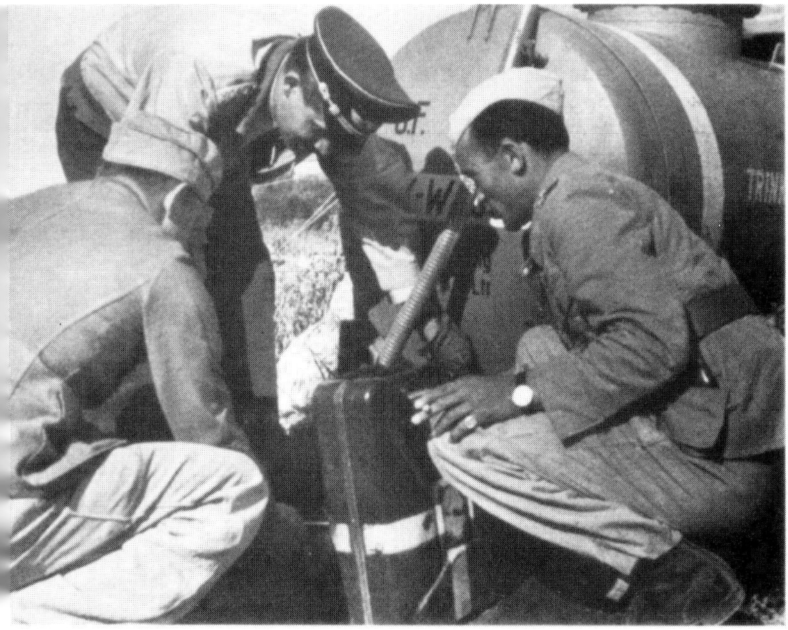

"Edu" Neumann, commander of I/JG-27, was Galland's closest friend since they served together in the Condor Legion in Spain. In this photo he is giving the General's Dachshund a drink of water. In June 1942, Neumann took over the wing from Colonel Woldenga and led it successfully during the most critical operations in Africa and subsequently in Italy.

One of the tasks of the General of the Fighter Arm was to evaluate the operability of new weapons and introduce them to the troops. At the Rechlin Test Center, a new weapons system is demonstrated in the presence of the Reichsmarshall.

On 19 August 1942 the British landing near Dieppe was repulsed. A landing force consisting mainly of Canadian troops came ashore under a massive air umbrella. Some 4,350 men, plus tanks, were involved. The landing, code-name "Jubilee," was conducted to demonstrate to the Russians that the Western Allies were ready to take major steps to relieve the German pressure on the Eastern Front. This dress rehearsal for the subsequent invasion turned out to be expensive for the Allies. JG-26, Galland's former wing, particularly distinguished itself in beating back the invasion. Here, Galland inspects destroyed landing boats and tanks on the beaches in Dieppe.

In fall of 1942 the General of the Fighter Arm called a major conference in the Air Ministry in Berlin. All the fighter wing *Kommodores* and group commanders were invited. The critical situation on all fronts required regrouping of the Jagdgeschwadern. JG-27, still operational in Africa, was increasingly unable to support the *Afrika Korps* due to lack of spares. Additional units were to be transferred to the south. At the same time, the Allied Air Force's numerical superiority was steadily increasing. Additional fighter units had to be organized and made operational. On the Eastern Front, the Fighter Arm was scattered, directed from one brush-fire to another, unable to concentrate forces in any one sector. The seriousness of the situation was clearly reflected in the grim expressions of the participants.

Mass production of the new FW-190 had started. The Focke-Wulf plants worked day and night to supply the fighter wings with this outstanding new aircraft.

30 October 1942: Adolf Galland's youngest brother, Lieutenant Paul Galland, was killed during aerial combat with Spitfires. The Third Group of JG-26, under Captain Priller, was escorting a fighter-bomber strike against Canterbury. On its way back, the group was attacked by Spitfires and the young lieutenant was shot down when he went to the aid of a comrade. Galland had a deep relationship with his youngest brother, and his death was a heavy blow. This photograph shows PG (left) with Captain Priller in front of a captured tracked vehicle. This photograph is probably the last photograph taken before PG's death.

General Galland in the company of highly-decorated wing commanders at *Wolfsschanze.* The General of the Fighter Arm receives a third set of the diamonds on this occasion. There is an amusing background to this event. On 28 January 1942, Galland was awarded the first diamonds. Later, during a meeting in his special train, the Reichsmarshall recognized that the decoration which Galland was wearing wasn't set with real diamonds but with chips. Goring, not only an admirer but an expert on precious stones, promised Galland a replacement with real diamonds. Very soon afterwards, Galland received a second example of the decoration in Karinhall. Goring also informed Hitler that a higher quality of diamonds had to be used for the highest German decoration for bravery. Unaware that Galland had already received a perfect replacement set from Goring, Hitler had another set made and presented it to Galland when this photograph was made. Sometime later, after a serious quarrel with Goring, Galland refused to wear this decoration any further and draped it around the neck of a stuffed game bird decorating his office in Berlin. A subsequent air-raid on Berlin destroyed not only the building but also the stuffed game bird and the decoration. When Hitler was informed of this, Adolf Galland then received the fourth set, which is the only one still in his possession.
In the above photograph, in addition to Galland, who is being decorated by Hitler, one sees Colonel Peltz, Lieutenant Colonel Lutzow, Major Wilke and Major Oesau.

Christmas 1942 was celebrated by Galland in the company of his old fighter wing on the Western Front. Major General Galland (promoted to that rank on 19 November 1942) felt happy in the circle of his old friends. From left to right seated at the table are Lieutenant Horten, Captain Michel, Captain Priller, A.G., Lieutenant Borris and Captain Causin.

During the Christmas holiday, Galland also met his old friend, Navy Commander and Surgeon, Dr. Heim, at Kortrijk. Dr. Heim had plenty of opportunities to demonstrate his surgical skills during the time that Galland led JG-26 on the Channel front. In the middle of the photograph is Captain "Pips" Priller, who was to assume command of JG-26 shortly after this photo was taken.

On 7 May 1943 the battle of North Africa was over and the totally exhausted German fighter units pulled back from Tunisia to Sicily. General Galland arrived on the island, greeted by Major General Osterkamp, at that time the commander of German fighter forces in Italy.

This photo shows Gunter Lutzow, promoted to colonel on 1 April 1943, talking to the general in Sicily. "Franzl" Lutzow, an experienced fighter commander, later was named Inspector of the German Fighter Forces in the South.

May 22, 1943, a day which Adolf Galland will never forget. With the approval of Field Marshal Milch, Prof. Messerschmitt invites Galland to test fly the prototype Me-262. In his book, *The First And The Last*, Galland describes in detail his difficulties in handling the prototype Me-262 which was fitted with a tail wheel rather than the nose wheel found on the production aircraft. The flight characteristics, the handling and the speed of the jet aircraft excited Galland as much as the other pilots who flew the jet later on.

Lechfeld Airbase near Munich. Designers, engineers and staff officers meet to witness the general's test flight and to hear his opinion of the aircraft.

Messerschmitt's Chief Test Pilot, Flight-Captain Fritz Wendel and Dr. Lusser, one of the Me-262 designers, review the aircraft in detail with Galland.

Galland's takeoff and subsequent evaluation of the jet fighter went like clock work. After the landing, Galland's enthusiastic comment became legendary, "It's as if an angel were pushing you."

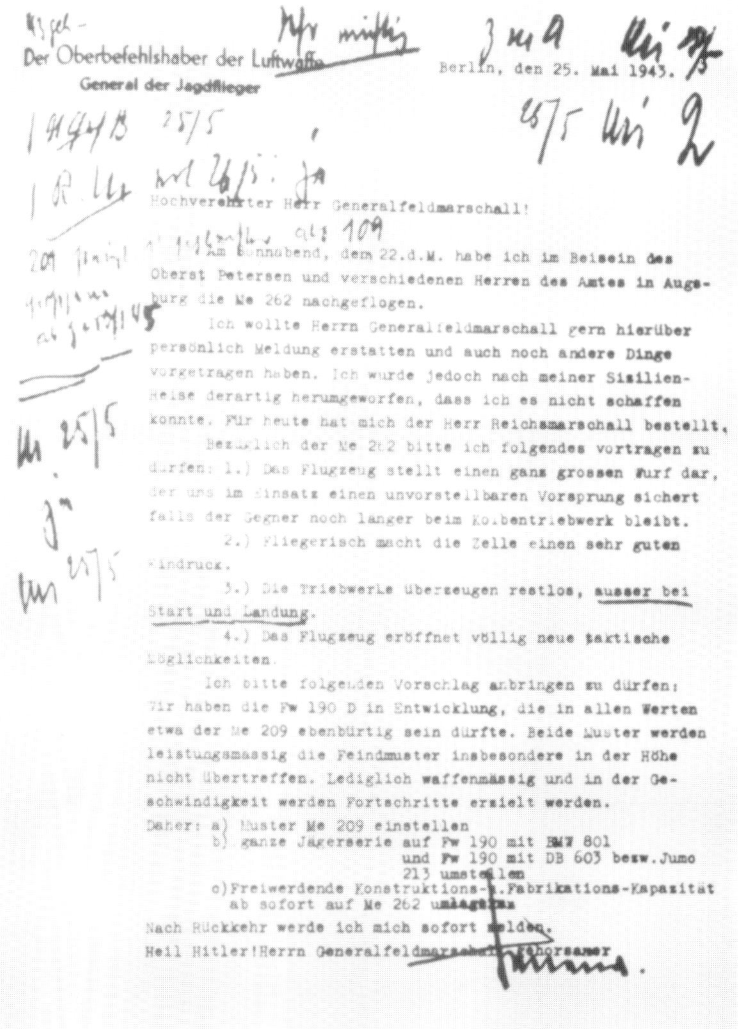

Der Oberbefehlshaber der Luftwaffe
General der Jagdflieger

Berlin, den 25. Mai 1943.

Hochverehrter Herr Generalfeldmarschall!

Am Sonnabend, dem 22.d.M. habe ich im Beisein des Oberst Petersen und verschiedenen Herren des Amtes in Augsburg die Me 262 nachgeflogen.

Ich wollte Herrn Generalfeldmarschall gern hierüber persönlich Meldung erstatten und auch noch andere Dinge vorgetragen haben. Ich wurde jedoch nach meiner Sizilien-Reise derartig herumgeworfen, dass ich es nicht schaffen konnte. Für heute hat mich der Herr Reichsmarschall bestellt.

Bezüglich der Me 262 bitte ich folgendes vortragen zu dürfen: 1.) Das Flugzeug stellt einen ganz grossen Wurf dar, der uns im Einsatz einen unvorstellbaren Vorsprung sichert falls der Gegner noch länger beim Kolbentriebwerk bleibt.

2.) Fliegerisch macht die Zelle einen sehr guten Eindruck.

3.) Die Triebwerke überzeugen restlos, ausser bei Start und Landung.

4.) Das Flugzeug eröffnet völlig neue taktische Möglichkeiten.

Ich bitte folgenden Vorschlag anbringen zu dürfen: Wir haben die Fw 190 D in Entwicklung, die in allen Werten etwa der Me 209 ebenbürtig sein dürfte. Beide Muster werden leistungsmässig die Feindmuster insbesondere in der Höhe nicht übertreffen. Lediglich waffenmässig und in der Geschwindigkeit werden Fortschritte erzielt werden.

Daher: a) Muster Me 209 einstellen
b) ganze Jägerserie auf Fw 190 mit BMW 801 und Fw 190 mit DB 603 bezw.Jumo 213 umstellen
c) Freiwerdende Konstruktions-u.Fabrikations-Kapazität ab sofort auf Me 262 umlagern

Nach Rückkehr werde ich mich sofort melden.

Heil Hitler! Herrn Generalfeldmarschall gehorsamer

Galland's report of 25 May 1943 to Field Marshal Milch described his first flight with the Me-262. His report also contained proposals for establishing priorities for future production of the fighter. Hitler's unbelievable decision to use the aircraft as a "Blitzbomber" turned the best fighter in the world into perhaps the world's worst bomber.

The commander of II/JG-26, Captain W.F. "Wutz" Galland, is awarded the Knight's Cross after 41 aerial victories on the Western Front. The date is 8 May 1943. The new *Kommodore,* Major Priller, is putting the decoration around his commander's neck. In the picture from the right, Lieutenant V. Donner, a friend of the Gallands, who died in combat on 8 March 1944 after scoring three aerial victories.

Two good friends; "Wutz" Galland and Lieutenant Ebersberger, leader of the Fourth Squadron, also an excellent pilot and commander. He too died in aerial combat on 24 October 1943 after scoring 27 aerial victories.

JG-26 also tested 21 centimeter (8½ inch) air-to-air rockets in 1943. It was intended that these weapons would be used to break up the US bomber formations which were penetrating German air space in increasing numbers. The rocket launcher tubes were open at the rear to avoid any recoil when being fired. The empty launching tube could be jettisoned afterwards. The tests were discontinued after it was found that the fighters compromised their maneuverability while carrying the heavy rockets. In this photograph the *Kommodore* and his group commanders discuss the advantages and disadvantages of the new weapon. Third from the left is Captain Galland.

After his promotion to major, "Wutz" Galland took off on his last mission on 17 August 1943. The second group, numbering 20 aircraft, attacked a large bomber formation escorted by approximately 200 fighters. The bombers were on their way back to England. As the group tried to gain on the bombers it was, in turn, attacked from behind and below by several Thunderbolts. Major Galland was killed in the subsequent air battle, and was buried in the cemetery of St. Trond in the presence of his parents, brother, and Colonel Priller.

Headquarters of the General of the Fighter Arm located in the Berlin Olympic Stadium. Colonel Mettig briefs the general on the situation in southern Italy. Fighter Wings 53 and 77 were now carrying the main burden of the air defense of the south.

November 1943 - General Galland is summoned by Goring to *Karinhall* to report on the situation, accompanied by Colonel Gunther von Maltzahn. Following the Allied landing in Italy, American bomber formations now penetrate German territory from the South. The relationship between the Reichsmarshall and Galland deteriorates day by day. Serious differences build between the two.

General Galland talking to Colonel Petersen, Chief of the Air Force Test Centers.

Galland's personal transport, a Siebel, Si-104, was decorated with the insignias of all the fighter units he visited. Easily recognized is the wolf's head of the twin-engine fighter unit, the insignia of JG-3 *Udet,* as well as the winged sword of JG-52. Later, as air superiority of Germany was lost, Galland used a fully armed FW-190 for his inspection tours.

At Lechfeld, the general meets Professor Messerschmitt, creator of a new generation of aircraft, and Captain Wolfgang Spate, head of Test Group 16. Spate reports on the successful preliminary tests of the world's first rocket fighter, the Me-163. In Insterburg, the Me-262 is demonstrated to Hitler in the hope that he will authorize its immediate production for the fighter arm. Hitler's decision to modify it into the Me-262 "Blitzbomber," Hitler's decision to modify it into the Me-262 "Blitzbomber," bitterly disappoints the German Fighter Command. The limited "Blitzbomber" missions are militarily useless while depriving German air defense of the badly-needed new fighter.

Spring 1944. General Galland welcomes fighter commanders to his headquarters in Berlin. Colonel Trautloft, Inspector of East Fighter forces, introduces Major von Kornataki, creator of *Sturmjager,* the commander of II/JG-11, Captain Krupinski, and Captain Albrecht, commander of II/ZG-1.

From left to right: Colonel Hannes Trautoft, General Galland, Major Kowalewski, commander of ZG-76, and Major Hohagen, commander of JG-27. Kowalewski later on lead the first jet bomber wing, KG-76, which would be equipped with the new Arado 234. Hohagen flew with Galland in JG-44 at the end of the war.

While flying an inspection tour in the spring of 1944, Galland was able to shoot down a 4-engined bomber, and was chased "all the way home" by a pack of angry Mustangs.

The mission of Test Group 25, commanded by Captain Horst Geyer, was to evaluate large-caliber weapons and other equipment to combat the U.S. bombers. Many ideas were proposed by the civil population. Special weapons such as the 3cm cannon, 21cm rockets and delayed action bombs received their final tests with this group before being released to the field. In June 1944, Captain Geyer took over the Me-262 Command and Major Christl replaced him. Renamed Fighter Group 10, this unit consisted of three squadrons of different aircraft types.

The weapons could now be evaluated in actual combat. At Rechlin Christl developed launching racks for the 5cm R4-m rocket, but the heavy weapon was introduced far too late to be of any military significance.

Colonel Lutzow is seen between General Galland and Captain Geyer. The small photo shows Major Christl.

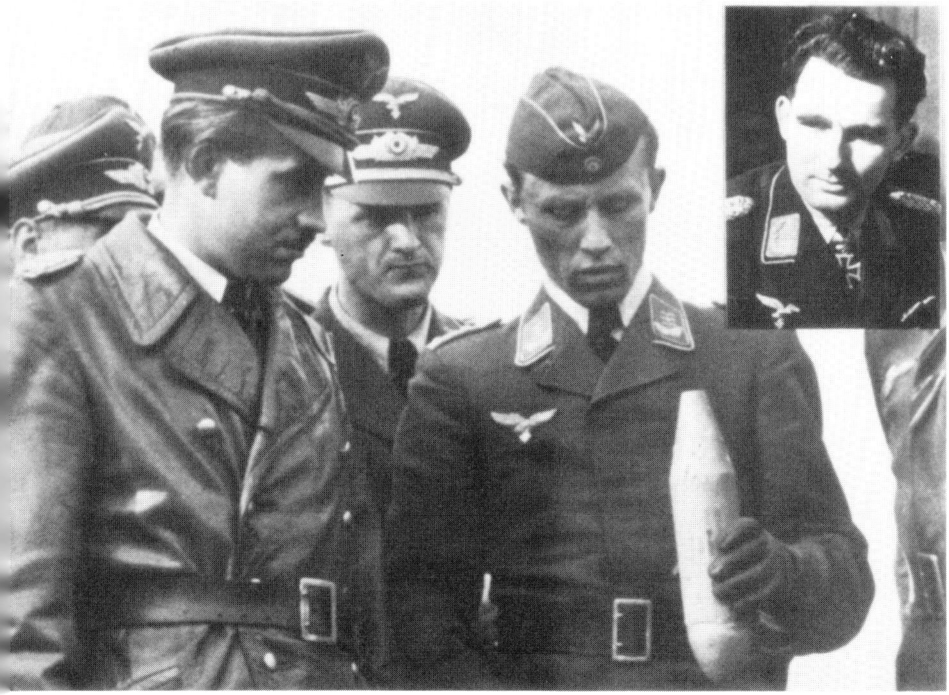

General Galland briefing the weapons industry production directors. In the background the Minister of Weapons Production, Albert Speer.

Fighters, fighters, more fighters was the most urgent requirement. The heavy losses of the units defending Germany had to be replaced and new units were to be created and held in reserve. Although the Allies attacked aircraft production plants without letup, the increased production goals were met. Aircraft production was moved underground into abandoned mines and tunnels, the aircraft assembled in large underground halls. In 1944, production of the Me-109 doubled as compared with the previous year. Focke Wulf 190 production tripled. However, high rate production of the Me-262 could not be achieved.

In 1943 fighter production was placed under the control of *Hauptdienstleiter* Saur. One year later a specification was drawn up for a *Volksjager*. The Heinkel factory was awarded the contract with the order to submit its engineering proposal within 12 days; 69 days later the final engineering drawings were delivered, and the first flight of the He-162 occurred on 6 December 1944.

Galland often visited Professor Kurt Tank, accompanied by his inspectors of day and night fighters, Trautloft and Streib. The Luftwaffe constantly called for better and faster aircraft. Tank not only designed the four-engined FW-200 and the FW-190, but was also the designer of the promising Ta-152, Ta-154 and numerous other projects.

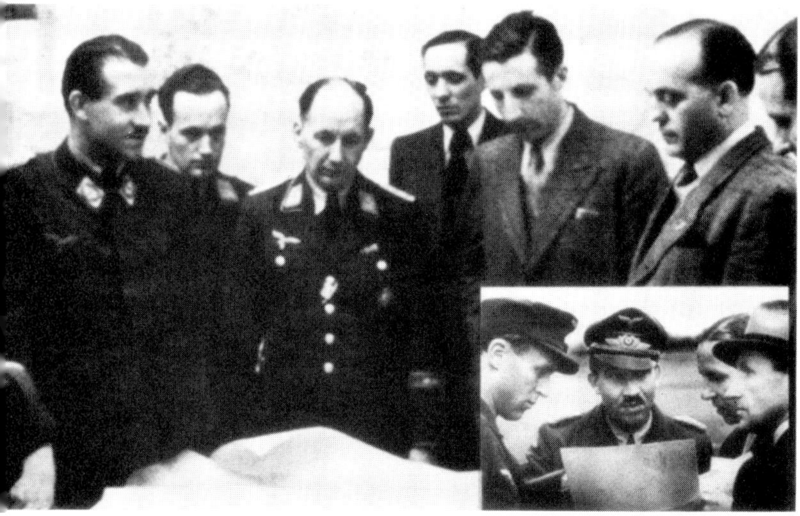

Tank's design offices were evacuated to Bad Eilsen where Galland continued frequent follow-up visits and flight tests the new aircraft.

On 11 May 1944 the German Air Force lost one of its famous fighter pilots, Colonel Walter Oesau, *Kommodore* of JG-1. He was shot down during an air battle with Lightnings in the area west of Koblenz. Oesau scored 125 victories in some 330 missions. In addition to 44 victories in the East, he shot down 73 aircraft on the Western Front, including ten four-engined bombers.

In Meldorf/ Holstein, Oesau's home town, the popular *Kommodore* is buried. General Galland salutes his dead comrade.

In the summer of 1944, General Galland visited the new heavy fighter-wing ZG-76 which was set up in August of 1943. The Me-110, 210 and 410 aircraft were equipped with 21cm rockets and heavy cannons (3.7 and 5cm). Despite this armament, losses against the Allied bomber formations were so catastrophic that the unit was dissolved. The pilots were retrained on the single-seat Fw-190 fighter and reassigned to JG-6.

The photograph of an Me-262 during takeoff marks a new era which can be considered as one of the most frustrating of the air war. Hitler's decision of November 1943 to downgrade the Me-262 into a "Blitzbomber" effectively ended the aircraft's last chance to change the air war. In May 1944, Hitler ordered the test of the "Blitzbomber" concept by means of operational missions. The first wing, KG-51, commanded by Major Schenk, was assigned the mission. However, almost secretly, the group under Captain Thierfelder, based at Lechfeld, began to use the Me-262 as a fighter. Soon, that group began to register significant victories. The immediate success of this small group finally convinced Goring to set up a larger fighter unit under the command of Major Walter Nowotny. This unit was in fact titled "the Nowotny Command."

This photograph, made at Lechfeld in early July 1944, marks the visit of Field Marshal Milch, Lieutenant Colonel Bohlan, General Galland; at the far right, Captain Thierfelder and next to him, Colonel Petersen.

Summer 1944 - accompanied by Colonel Trautloft, General Galland visits his old fighter wing on the western front. Leutenant Colonel Priller, Kommodore of JG-26, leads his guests across the airfield. The external appearance of the base has changed. Aircraft revetments and crew accomodations are camouflaged in the surrounding forest. The sharp eyes of Allied reconnaissance aircraft and the constant presence of hostile fighter-bombers force these precautionary measures.

On 24 August 1944, First Lieutenant Erich Hartmann became the highest-scoring fighter pilot of the German Air Force by reaching a record total of 301 victories. On 25 August Hartmann was awarded the diamonds to his cross and simultaneously forbidden to engage in further combat. Together with Galland, Hartmann visited Reichsmarshall Goring and requested reinstatement to combat status. After a commander's training course in Konigsberg, Hartmann returned to his wing on 1 November as captain and commander of the First Group of JG-52. As Galland had earlier done, Goring also refused to wear his iron cross, which is the reason for the unusual angle from which this photograph is taken.

On 7 and 8 November, General Galland and General Keller visited the Me-262 Nowotny fighter command near Osnabruck. Nowotny's unit consisted of two Me-262 squadrons stationed at Achmer and Hesepe. Both airfields were located precisely in the center of the main "corridor" used by the Allied bomber and fighter formations. In the beginning the bases suffered heavily from repeated attacks by fighters and fighter-bombers. Then, as the bases received FW 190 defensive fighters, the jet pilots were able to take off and land in relative safety. Major Walter Nowotny, an outstanding and talented pilot, had scored his 250th victory on the eastern front on 14 October 1943. This earned him the diamonds to his cross on October 1943. General Galland commented on Nowotny as follows: "he was the best I had for the Me-262 command." Flying ability, courage, prudence and a talent for organization and empathy were happily melded in this young (23-year-old) major from Austria.

In the early afternoon of 8 November 1944, Major Nowotny took off on his second mission of the day. His wingman had to abandon the takeoff because of an engine fire. Nowotny continued the mission alone. After shooting down a hostile aircraft (victory 258) the Me-262 "white 8" dived vertically out of the clouds and moments later a powerful explosion marked the end of this outstanding pilot and human being. It was a bitter shock not only for the witnesses but for all the German fighter pilots. As was later learned, his death was even noted with regret by the Allied fighter pilots. Galland, one of the witnesses, lost another of his very best officers. The success of the Nowotny Command contributed essentially to Hitler's decision to finally authorize the formation of the first jet fighter wing.

Colonel Steinhoff was authorized to set up a new jet fighter wing. Test pilots and specialists from the Lechfeld Test Center and the Nowotny Command formed the core of the group. In addition, high-scoring pilots from other fighter wings applied for transfer to this unit. By February, the First and the Third Groups started operations. The Second Group was formed in February but saw no combat.

The aerodynamically successful form of this new fighter aircraft is clearly seen in this photograph. The pilots nicknamed this new aircraft the "Turbo."

Hitler ordered some Me-262s equipped with a KWK-5 tank cannon of 5 centimeter caliber. His reasoning was that the tanks started their offensive fire at a longer range than that of the aircraft. He completely overlooked the simple fact that the Me-262 in flight presented a far worse weapons platform than the tank. The operational tests were a disaster and the program was quickly cancelled.

JV-44

After Galland's dismissal as general of the fighter arm, Hitler cancelled the order forbidding Galland to engage in combat and ordered the formation of a new iet fighter unit. The "Turbo Fighter Group 44" led by General Galland, consisted of highly-dedicated officers and many group commanders who had fallen into disfavor. The group was set up in Brandenburg-Briest and transferred to Munich-Riem on 31 March. From that base, Galland and his squadron-mates flew the last missions of a war which was already lost.

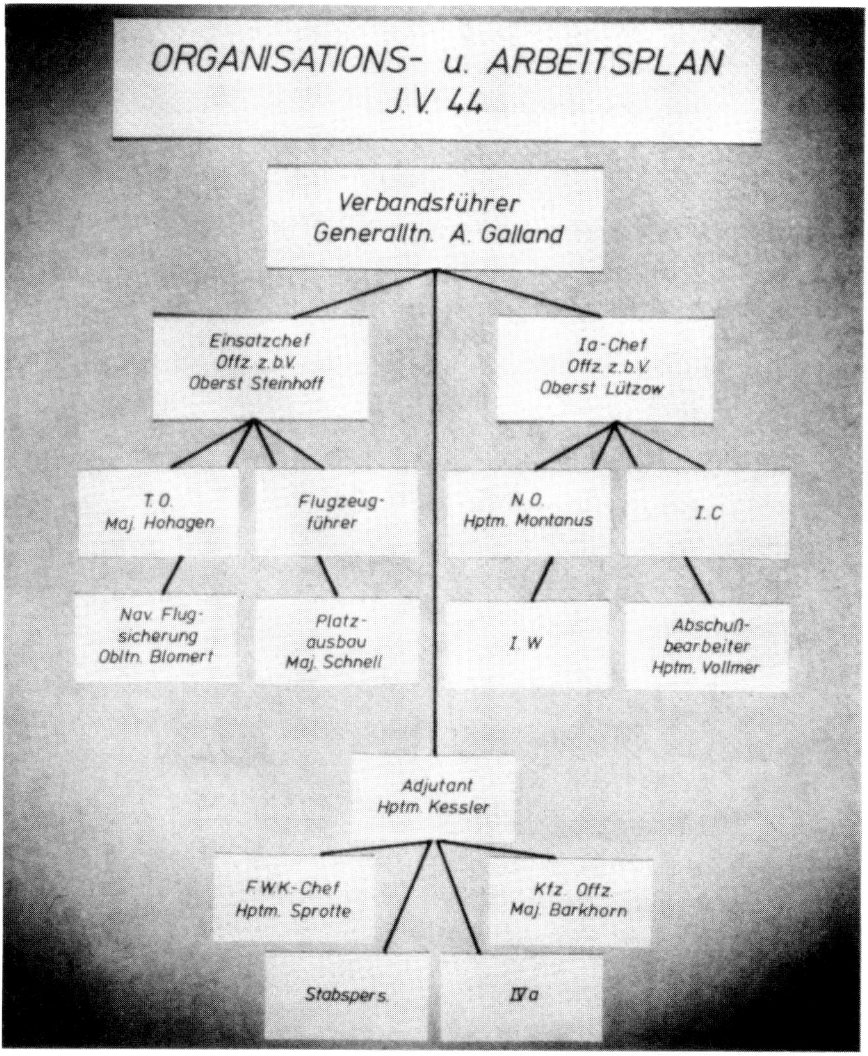

The proud birds lined up as if on parade. Very soon, this lineup was no longer possible even at Munich.

The operations chief of the fighter unit, Colonel Steinhoff at the telephone surrounded by his friends. Behind Steinhoff stands Colonel Lutzow, to his left Majors Barkhorn and Krupinski.

The fighter pilots of JV-44 during a simple luncheon. Colonel Steinhoff is sitting in the middle of the group.

Once again, Steinhoff together with his wingman, Lieutenant Fahrmann. On 18 April 1945 Steinhoff crashed during takeoff, sustaining serious injuries and severe burns. (lower photograph) The smoking remains of Steinhoff's Me-262 shortly after the crash. Adolf Galland, who personally led this mission, had very little hope that his friend would survive.

The last photo of Colonel Gunther, Lutzow. Galland and "Franzel," very close friends by that time, on their way towards their "Turbos" on the Munich-Riem airfield. Lutzow disappeared on 24 April 1945 near Donauworth, when radio contact with his Me-262 was suddenly interrupted, never to be re-established.

The desperate and bitter days and weeks left their imprint on Galland's face.

On 26 April 1945, Adolf Galland took off from Munich-Riem on his last mission. The five-aircraft formation sighted a Marauder group near Newburg on the Danube River and attacked. In his excitement, Galland forgot to arm his R-4M rockets but the four 3cm cannons destroyed a bomber, which exploded in the air. A second bomber was also hit. A Thunderbolt suddenly sighted the Me-262 in front of him. Galland felt a sharp impact on his knee. The cabin and instrument panel exploded into wreckage, and he felt the right engine taking hits. Putting his 262 into a dive, Galland outdistanced the pursuing aircraft and landed his crippled fighter on the Munich airfield. A bomb crater provided the wounded pilot with shelter as the airfield was immediately attacked by Thunderbolts.
The painting by Frank Wootton, made in 1979, depicts the situation just after the second attack on the Marauder formation.

The Thunderbolt was flown by Lieutenant Jim Finnegan of San Rafael, California, with whom Galland became a friend in 1979. Galland also met one of the Marauder gunners in Salt Lake City who parachuted to safety. He was the only survivor of that crew. Fragments of the downed Marauder were found by a magnetic detector years later and sent to Galland by some Neuburg residents.

After Galland was wounded, Lieutenant Colonel Heinz Bar assumed command of JV-44, now consisting of about 60 "turbos," and transfered it to Salzburg and Innsbruck, which become the final bases of this unique group. On 3 May 1945, as the sound of approaching American tanks was clearly heard, the remaining aircraft of JV-44 were put to the torch. For the fighter pilot elite of this unit, this marked the end of the war and the beginning of a new period as prisoners of war. The wounded Galland was brought to the military hospital at Tegernsee.

On 8 May 1945, after the German surrender, Galland was interrogated in Heidelberg by USAF Major Tobias Van Rossum-Daum. Many years afterwards - in August 1979 - Galland once again met with Van Rossum-Daum and his son, USAF Captain Tobias Van Rossum-Daum, Jr. They become friends.

American Interrogation

HEADQUARTERS
344TH BOMB GROUP, AAF
APO 206, U S ARMY

14 May, 1945

PRELIMINARY INTERROGATION REPORT OF ONE OF THE GAF'S MOST FAMOUS PILOTS --- GALLAND (GENERAL OF THE FIGHTERS)

PREAMBLE:

1. Towards the end of the struggle, and after he had been dismissed from his post as General der Jagdflieger (General of the Fighters) he received reluctant approval from Goring to form a unit which was variously known as Jagd Verband 44 (officially) or "Galland" Verband. The organization was built up with some of the GAF most experienced pilots and ground personnel, and when it became obvious that surrender was inevitable, Galland gave orders for a mass surrender, as a unit. Contact was established with I TAC, and arrangements had been made, but for two days weather closed in over Salzburg and Innsbruck and thus delayed the show never came off. Instead, land forces over-ran the area and General Galland, who had been wounded on 26 April, and the airfields used by his unit and his personnel stationed there were taken by elements of the US Seventh Army.

LAST BATTLE:

2. On 26 April 1945, at about 1100 hours, Galland took off from Munchen/Riem with five other ME 262s of his Jagdverband 44. One returned with engine trouble. Their mission was to attack a formation of B-26 Marauders flying in two tight Vics of about 30 aircraft each. Coming from 12 o'clock the German fighters passed over the formation and wheeled around in a dive for an attack from

about 8 o'clock from below. Galland, with his Katchsmarek (his number two) who was an inexperienced young non-com, had picked the outside rear flying B-26 of the Vie as his target. As they closed in, the B-26 formation recognized them and opened fire before the Germans did. Galland pulled up and fired his cannons. The B-26 exploded in mid-air. Meanwhile Galland, bypassing the exploded aircraft, lined up on the second, but since he failed to release the safety button for his rockets, they did not go off, and he obtained only a few cannon hits on his second target.

WE ALMOST GOT HIM:

3. While banking away to observe the results of his atack on the second B-26, he sustained hits in the fuel tanks from that bomber. At the same moment he was jumped by a US fighter (Galland did not observe if it was a Thunderbolt or a Mustang), who attacked from above and the rear. His aircraft was hit several times in the cockpit, and the jet engines. Galland himself sustained splinters in his right leg thus incapacitated, and with his instrument board shot out, he dove straight down to get away from his attacker. Not pursued, Galland then followed the Autobahn to Munchen/Riem, to find upon his arrival there that Mustangs were attacking the flight strip. Because his aircraft was badly hit, and because he had lost control over the speed of his jet engines, he had to turn the fuel off, and make a tree-top glide approach. He was able to land without being attacked once more.

4. The result of his encounter, according to Galland, was four aircraft shot down, either four B-26s, or three B-26s and one Mustang. Losses were one Me 262 shot down, but pilot safe. (These claims agree in general with the losses of 42nd Bomb Wing and of First Tactical Air Force. Official records show that three B-26s were shot down, plus one B-26, crash-landed behind our lines due to enemy action.

JAGD VERBAND 44:

8. In forming his unit, General Galland was determined to gather around him the very best that the GAF could offer. It was known in GAF circles that if you wanted to belong to the Jagdverband 44, you had to have at least the Ritterkreuz (Knights' Cross). This plan had been opposed by Goring and General Pelz, and Galland had to fight

them all along, but nevertheless succeeded in getting only the top-notch pilots.

DETAILS OF PRISONER:

14. This GAF ace flew every American fighter used in this theatre (including the P-39). He was invited to test captured Allied aircraft. In his capacity as General of fighters, he also flew the latest models and new aircraft developed by the GAF. From American aircraft he chose the Mustang as the best fighter. Of US bombers, Galland considered the B-26s flying usually in tight formations were very difficult to approach. He found through hard experience that they had devastating power.

15. Galland had a rather spectacular career in the GAF. At the outbreak of the war in 1939, he was a Oberlieutenant (1st Lt.). After becoming Captain, he was promoted in 1940 to Major and then Lt. Col. The next year he became Oberst (Col.) and exactly a year later he became General Major (Brigadier General). His final promotion to General Lieutenant (Major General) occured in November 1944.

16. Galland wears the highest decoration of the German Armed Forces; The Knights Cross with Oakleaves, with Swords and Diamonds.

GENERALLIEUTENANT ADOLF GALLAND, born 19.3.1912

M. VAN ROSSUM-DAUM
MAJOR, AIR CORPS.
INTERROGATOR.

Being a prisoner of war for two years, the former General of the Fighter Arm had to face more than 100 interrogations. Captain Jack Whitten - on the left -intelligence officer and interpretor, became a friend of POW Galland.

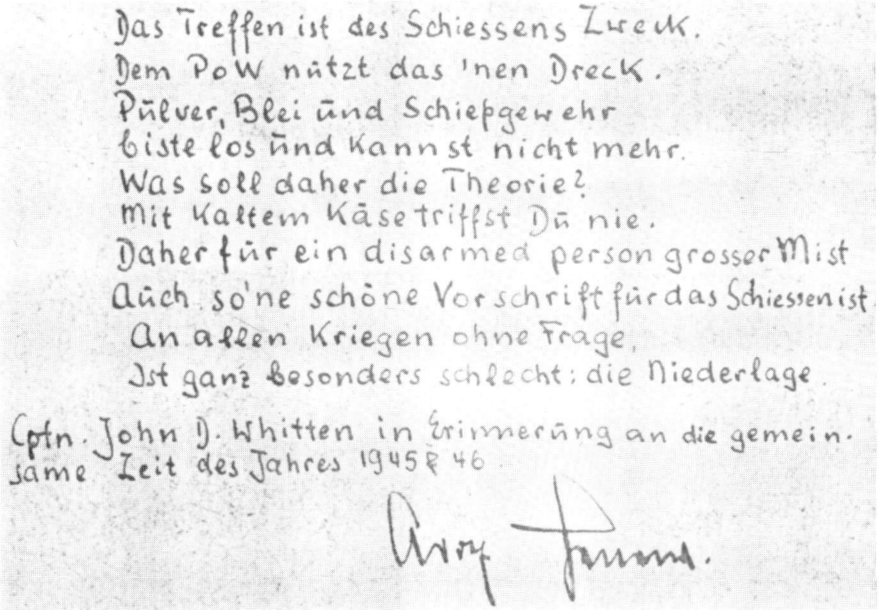

Das Treffen ist des Schiessens Zweck.
Dem PoW nützt das 'nen Dreck.
Pulver, Blei und Schießgewehr
biste los und kannst nicht mehr.
Was soll daher die Theorie?
Mit kaltem Käse triffst Du nie.
Daher für ein disarmed person grosser Mist
Auch so'ne schöne Vorschrift für das Schiessen ist.
An allen Kriegen ohne Frage,
Ist ganz besonders schlecht: die Niederlage.

Cptn. John D. Whitten in Erinnerung an die gemeinsame Zeit des Jahres 1945 & 46

Galland and other German officers are brought back aboard of a B-17 from Engiand to Kaufbeuren after lengthy interrogations were terminated.

During his time as POW the "prominent prisoner" received permission from the Americans to visit his parents. "Leave on word of honor" - a proof of confidence. The photos shows Adolf Galland with his parents at Westerholt.

Argentinian Interlude

After release from POW camp, the former general tried his best to find work. There was no chance to start flying again, so he chose a job close to his hobby: hunting. He became an assistant forest ranger. Shown here is his work permit.

ARBEITS-PASS

Nr. 90R/6488 Personal-Ausweis Nr. AJ 1o1896 UCW

Familienname: Galland Vorname: Adolf

bei Frauen auch Geburtsname

geboren am: 19.März 1912

Geburtsort: Westerholt Westf.

Familienstand: led., ~~verh., gesch., verw.~~

Wohnung: Lehmkuhlen Kr.Plön

Erlernter Beruf: Verkehrsflieger

Berufs-Gruppe 2

Beschäftigt als: Forsthelfer

und -Art R 4

Dienstsiegel

Eigenhändige Unterschrift

ausgestellt am: 4/3.48

ARBEITSAMT

Unterschrift

Unselbständige Arbeitnehmer (grau) Männer

Galland couldn't resist an offer made by the Argentine Government to work for its air force as a consultant. AG says in his book, "Even if Argentina had offered German pilots nothing but the accomplishment of their desire to fly again, almost nobody would have refused the offer. Flying is more than sport and more than a profession. Flying is pure passion and desire, which absorbs a complete life." Galland is seen aboard the Italian liner *Andrea C,* clay-pigeon shooting. Even during the passage to Argentina, the restless Galland was active.

In the suburbs of Buenos Aires is located the wonderful garden-town of El Palomar. Here Galland moved into a house and started his new life. The photo shows him, with his German-speaking liaison officer and friend, Captain Luis Grieben, while delivering a lecture to Argentine Air Force officers.

Galland talking with the famous aircraft designer, Professor Kurt Tank, who also worked for the Argentine Government. Together with his German and Argentine colleagues, Tank designed and built, in Cordoba, the *Pulqui II* jet fighter. On 8 February 1951 the jet was presented to the President, General Peron, at the airport in Buenos Aires.

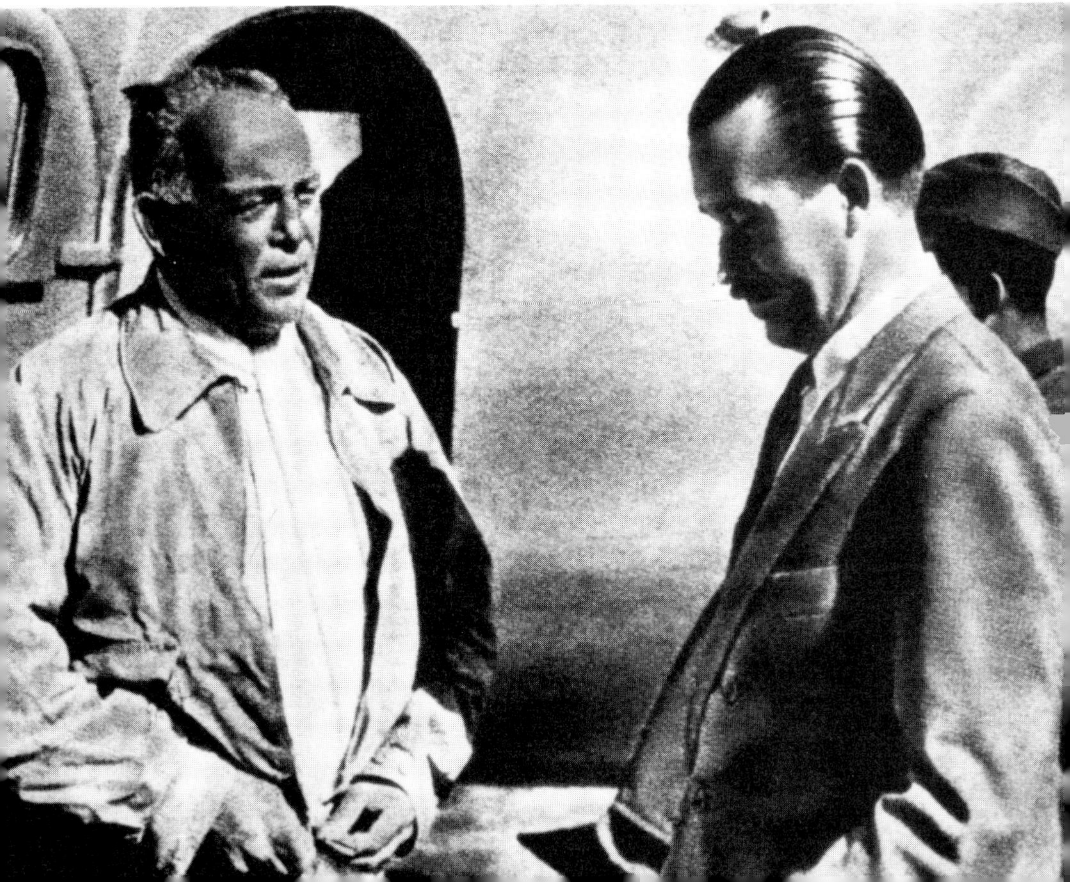

For the first time, after the war, Daimler-Benz participated in a major international automobile race. In February 1951 the South American continent was to be crossed in a road race. The photo shows, from left to right: Mercedes racing driver Lang; Mr. Zayn, the German founder of El Palomar; Galland and Mercedes racing driver Klein.

During the weekends, weather and season permitting, Galland could be found hunting in the Pampas. Here he is with a wild boar.

In 1952, in an Avro Lincoln, Galland flew with his Argentine fellow aviators to Tierra Del Fuego and deep into the Antarctic.

Galland was often a welcome guest of the "gauchos of the air." Here he is seen with a shepherd.

The numerous aviation clubs in the area allowed the enthusiastic pilot many opportunities to fly again.

In Argentina Galland met Sylvina Countess von Donhoff. Here, she watches Galland's pre-takeoff preparations with some concern.

Once again back in Germany. In 1953, Galland discussed the manuscript of his book, *The First and the Last,* with the publisher Franz Schneekluth. The brain-trust from the left: Erich Bindert, who found the publisher; a proof-reader from the publisher; Baroness Gisela von Donner; Franz Schneekluth and Adolf Galland in Darmstadt.

The former General of Fighters, who up to now had claimed to have neither the time nor the maturity for a harmonious marriage, changed his personal life style. On 12 February 1954 he married Countess von Donhoff, who became Mrs. Galland.

Werner Baumbach, a famous and popular German bomber pilot, lost his life in Argentina while testing the Henschel 293, a radio-controlled, powered glide bomb. Adolf Galland and other aviation friends escorted the coffin of the former colonel, whose body was transferred to Germany and buried in the small cemetery of Cloppenburg, his home-town.

At the request of the Argentine Government, Galland tested this Fiat jet trainer in Turin, Italy.

LICENCE 1

LICENZA

Fotografia del titolare

Firma del titolare: ....

La licenza internazionale di pilota di aerodina da turismo (secondo grado) (licence de pilote d'aérodynes de tourisme) *avente il n.* 5201

in data 26 APR. 1955

è stata rilasciata al Signor Galland Adolfo Ferdinando di Adolfo

il quale, con la presente licenza è autorizzato a pilotare i seguenti tipi di aerodina: indicati sul brevetto

La presente licenza è valida fino al 10 marzo 1956

A Roma *il* 26 APR. 1955 **19 A.**

(timbro)

p. IL MINISTRO

IL DIRETTORE CAPO DIVISIONE

(firma)

In June 1954, Galland participated in an international air rally in Italy. He needed an Italian pilot's license and the special permission of the military authorities to fly an Italian prototype, which was not yet fully certified. A most successful navigator was retired Colonel Edu Neumann, a close friend of Galland's. "Fritze" Dettmann, a well-known photo-reporter, belonged to the crew as well. The team flew a Piaggio 149.

A rather well-fed Italian is responsible for checking the empty and take off weight calculations.

The co-operation between pilot and navigator was remarkable despite the strong garlic smell from the right seat.

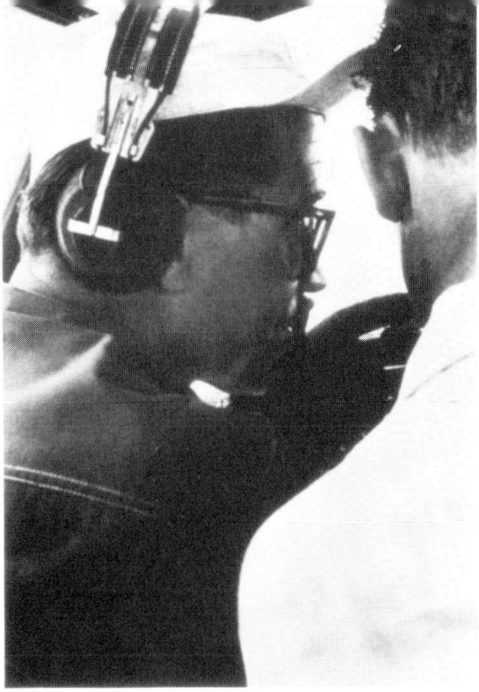

A nearly-satisfied Galland receives the second-place trophy. It was a hard fight to win this position, against strong international competition. And the Italians are very tricky competitors.

The smiling faces of some participating crews after the difficult competition.

Galland and Neumann leaving the reception given in honor of the winners and participants in the president's palace. During this very difficult air rally, two crews were lost in fatal crashes and seven planes were destroyed during a violent wind-storm in Rimini.

Back to Argentina - surrounded by Argentine flight officers in the province of Parana, "Vino de Honor" is offered to AG.

El Poder Ejecutivo Nacional

Buenos Aires, 7 de febrero de 1955.

Visto lo propuesto por el Ministro de Aeronáutica, y

CONSIDERANDO:

Que el Teniente General D. ADOLFO GALLAND ha servido durante siete años en la Fuerza Aérea Argentina, con su competencia universalmente reconocida, aportando a ella su valiosa experiencia de guerra;

Que los importantes servicios prestados a la misma en su leal tarea de asesoramiento y los numerosos trabajos realizados comprometen el reconocimiento de la Aeronáutica Argentina,

EL PRESIDENTE DE LA NACION ARGENTINA

D E C R E T A :

Artículo 1º - Otórgase el Título de Aviador Militar "Honoris Causa", al señor Teniente General D. ADOLFO GALLAND, perteneciente a la República Federal Alemana.

Artículo 2º - El Ministerio de Aeronáutica extenderá el correspondiente diploma y distintivo acreditantes.

Artículo 3º - La Dirección General del Personal de Aeronáutica hará las anotaciones correspondientes, inscribiendo al mencionado Oficial Superior en el Registro de Títulos "Honoris Causa", con copia del presente Decreto.

Artículo 4º - El presente Decreto será refrendado por los señores Ministros Secretarios de Estado en los Departamentos de Aeronáutica y Relaciones Exteriores y Culto.

Artículo 5º - Comuníquese, dése a la Dirección General del Registro Nacional, vuelva al Ministerio de Aeronáutica para su publicación en Boletín Aeronáutico Público y archívese en la Dirección General del Personal de Aeronáutica. - PERON. - Juan I. San Martín. - Jerónimo Remorino.

ES COPIA FIEL DEL DECRETO Nº 1613

7 February 1955; farewell to Argentina. Adolf Galland receives the military pilots wings and is thereby appointed to the title "Honorary Argentine military pilot." A decree was issued in appreciation of Galland's work with the Argentine Air Force.

Translation of the decree shown on the left side

Buenos Aires, 7 Feb. 1955

After acknowledgement of the proposal of the Minister of Aeronautics and considering that:

Lieutenant General Adolf Galland (Ret.) has worked with the Argentine Air Force during the past 7 years in an area of responsibility, which is generally respected, and furthermore has given freely of his valuable combat experience and donated his knowledge to the Air Force, in addition to various other activities which are properly acknowledged by the Argentine Air Force.

THE PRESIDENT OF THE ARGENTINE NATION
decrees the following

Article 1 *to award the title of a military pilot "Honoris Causa" to Lieutenant General Adolf Galland, (Ret.), citizen of the Federal Republic of Germany.*

Article 2 *The Minister of Aviation is to issue and to notarize the corresponding diploma.*

Article 3 *The Director General for Aeronautical Personnel is to publish the corresponding announcements and register the a.m. high officer in the list with the title "Honoris Causa" with a copy of this decree.*

Article 4 *This decree is to be signed by the Ministers of Aviation, Foreign Affairs and Cultural Affairs.*

Article 5 *The Office of the Director General of the National Register is to be so informed with the request to relay it thereupon to the Ministry of Aviation for publication in the official aeronautical bulletin and to make the necessary registrations in the archives of the office of the Director General for Aviation Personnel Affairs.*

PERON - Juan I. San Martin - Jeronimo Remorino

This is a true copy of decree No. 1613

(signature)
Juan Francisco Fabri
Brigadier General

The letter published on the next page, sent by the German Ambassador in Argentina to the Foreign Office in Bonn regarding Adolf Galland, was also an important factor in his preliminary selection by Mr. Blank for the position of the first CIC of the new Luftwaffe. However, Franz Josef Strauss, the first defense minister, brought along his own CIC from Munich and Galland stayed a civilian.

TRANSLATION

Buenos Aires, 13, Jan. 1955

EMBASSY OF THE FEDERAL REPUBLIC OF GERMANY
In Buenos Aires

To the
Foreign Office
53 Bonn

Ref.: General (ret.) Adolf Galland
Subj.: Report dated 7 Oct. 1954-212 No. 2736/54

General Galland has returned to Germany with his wife, the daughter of the former German Consul General, Count Donhoff.

In 1948, General Galland came to Argentina, together with Prof. Tank and his group, in order to work as consultant for the Air Ministry. The original four-year contract was repeatedly extended. First, he worked in the Recruiting District Headquarters, and thereafter as tactical consultant to the Air Defense Command.

In the first phase, he worked together with American and English delegations, which, however, were transferred back to their home countries, with the exception of some North Americans working as consultants with Argentine Naval Aviation. Therefore, Galland was the final foreign consultant who worked with the Argentine Air Force.

I have heard nothing but the highest praise and approval regarding Galland's activities and particularly from the side of the competent military authorities, he was highly respected.

This was also the reason for the cordial farewell which the Argentine people arranged for him. On the occasion of a military celebration he was awarded the title of "military pilot honoris causa."

An honor guard lined up at attention was reviewed by General Galland and the Commander in Chief of the Argentine Air Force. Then the government decree was read, in which Galland received the award; it included a detailed appreciation of General Galland's efforts on behalf of Argentine Air Defense. On the same day, the Commander in Chief of the Argentine Air Force gave a lunch in honor of General Galland, at which many high-ranking Argentine Air Force officers participated. On that occasion, CIC told me that General Galland and his activities were much appreciated in this country, especially since he maintained his role as a military consultant in Argentina, without involving himself in Argentina's political affairs.

It is a matter of fact that he avoided any kind of political involvement during his stay in Argentina. It was to be especially mentioned, that he had no association with Mr. Rudel, a political half-wit. Although General Galland was respected and frequently invited with his wife to social gatherings - despite his previous position and abilities - he has never pushed himself into the foreground.

General Galland told me that he will return to Germany hoping to work in a civil capacity, but he is also prepared and ready to be of assistance in case he is asked, to help build up the German Luftwaffe.

(Signed by German Ambassador Terdenge)

A New Start at Home 30 Years Thereafter

by Anton Weiler

In early 1955, Adolf Galland, now nearly 43 years of age, returned to Germany. Fully aware of the fact that the 40s are the decisive years in a man's life, he was determined to build a new livelihood. After a stay of seven years in Argentina, he left that country with the expressions of respect and friendship of the Argentinians still fresh in his mind. He returned with up-to-date knowledge and experience in the aviation field. Always self-critical, he now started a new life in Germany.

A short time after Galland's return from Argentina, he was asked to see Mr. Blank, at that time "the commissioner of the Federal Chancellor, responsible for the questions dealing with the increase of allied troops." Mr. Blank said that Galland was to become the first chief of the new German Air Force, which was about to be authorized. This was planned in the framework of the European Defense Community, but was still being blocked by the French in 1955. This was finally resolved when the Federal Republic of Germany became a member of NATO. However, the new Defense Minister, Franz-Josef Strauss, decided on General Josef Kammhuber, also from Munich, as leader of the Air Force.

In early 1955, Galland settled in Neuss. For two years he worked as an aerospace industry consultant with Messrs. Kichfeld in Dusseldorf. In late summer of 1957 Galland made another important decision in his life; he moved to Bonn and opened an office as an independent aerospace consultant. This decision is typical of his character, his talent and temper; he is an individualist, who wants to be the "number one" in any field of activity that interests him. Now he could use his knowledge and experience - together with much hard work, diligence and effort. Adolf Galland's knowledge and advice were desired and he started working as consultant to many aerospace companies based in Germany and abroad.

But Galland could not give up active flying. The first year after his return from Argentina, he participated in a flying display. In September 1955 he flew during the *Flugtag der Nationen* (Air Show of the Nations) in Dusseldorf, and two years later he competed in the *Deutschlandflug* (Germany Air Rally).

Galland's contact with former German fighter pilots, which was continued while in Argentina, became more and more intensive after his return. In October, 1956, the Association of Fighter Pilots nominated the former General of Fighter Arm to the post of Honorary Chairman.

Contacts with former enemies - in England, the United States and Canada - were initiated and deepened. His former enemies considered Adolf Galland the best-known German fighter pilot as well as a combat leader. Without any doubt he belongs to those personalities who enjoy a high reputation on both sides during WW II. His book *The First and the Last* - translated into 15 languages and selling over three million copies - helped make him even more well-known outside of Germany. The fact that Adolf Galland was able to grow from a successful fighter pilot to a successful senior air force commander - one of only a few men in airwar history - contributes to the respect and high esteem he enjoys among his former opponents.

He speaks the English language well enough that communication from one to the other gets a personal touch, which is essential to making friends. This led to the first German-American Fighter Pilots Meeting in Kirn, in 1961.

Celebrating his 50th birthday on 19 March 1962, the successful aerospace consultant made a dream come true! He bought an aircraft, a Beechcraft Bonanza affectionately called "The Fat One." Together they have logged more thn 1,000 flight hours. He used this aircraft in numerous air rallys, including the *Deutschlandflug*. In addition, he flies "The Fat One" on business and pleasure trips all over Europe.

Becoming a member of the IOC (International Order of Characters) was considered by Galland to be special recognition. The organization is a hand-picked group, numbering many famous aviation personalities among its members. Besides famous WW II pilots like Colonel Francis Gabreski from the US, the late Sir Douglas Bader, and Johnnie Johnson from Great Britain, it includes General Doolittle, Senator Goldwater, Prince Bernhard of the Netherlands, and astronauts Scott Carpenter and James McDivitt. The late "great old lady" of German aviation, Hanna Reitsch, was also a member of the group. Being closely connected with aviation, they all have a common interest.

All IOC members have nicknames, a pecularity of the association. For example, Adolf Galland carries the nickname "Red Knight" while General Steinhoff is called "Macky." Galland became a member of the IOC in 1961, and was nominated "Pilot of the Year" in 1963. In February 1973 he became an honorary lifetime member of the association.

In late 1961 a prominent German insurance company, the Gerling Group in Cologne, requested Galland to work as consultant while it expanded into various general aviation areas. The Gerling Group, with Galland's support, began building a network of short-haul feeder airlines and specialized charter operations.

Adolf Galland was intrigued by the many challenges of the expansion. The job was made to order for him since it required a consultant experienced in aero-technical, organizational and economic aspects. He took over this task with his analytical intelligence, his intensive special know-how and his inherently dynamic personality.

In 1965 - when those above-mentioned activities of the Gerling Group were concentrated in the Air Lloyd Group - Galland became Chairman of the Board of Directors of Air Lloyd. Crop-spraying by helicopter was launched and the company began working on contracts in Germany and abroad. Galland's earlier experience was in demand as the contract work expanded. He continues today as the chairman of the board of this group, still enthusiastically helping to monitor and expand the group's activities.

Also, in September 1963 the private life of the energetic, self-confident Adolf Galland, changed as he married for the second time. Spurred by the desire to find a home of his own, he bought a recently-built house at Oberwinter (near Bonn), which became the geographic center of his life. Quickly, two expansions grew this wonderfully situated house into a significant estate. Now AG could establish the kind of atmosphere which fitted his character and his way of life. In this house he welcomes his many German and foreign friends with pleasant hospitality.

The marriage to Hannelies Galland set the stage for a further pleasant event. A famous contemporary once listed the deeds which a man should accomplish in his life:

> to plant a tree,
> to write a book,
> to build a house,
> to create a son

The trees were planted by Galland during his early training as a forest ranger, the book had been written in Argentina and the house at Oberwinter was now also completed.

The "blessed event" became a fact on 7 November 1966, when his son Andreas-Hubertus was born. The "fourth deed" was fulfilled. His wife and his friends experienced a 54-year-old proud, happy and devoted daddy. A new generation was born to carry on the family name.

Favored by his typical luck, a daughter was born in July of 1969. And she, too, was baptized (like her brother earlier) by the "Flying Father" Schulte, with the name of Alexandra-Isabelle.

Adolf Galland's business commitments led him around the world. From February to March 1967 he visited Australia and New Zealand upon the request of VFW-Fokker, to evaluate the market potential for the first German post-war civil airliner project, the VFW-614.

In addition to Europe and South America, the USA and Africa were also of special interest to those firms he represented.

An intriguing, (but not too simple) additional task kept AG busy from 1967-1969. A British film-company, Spitfire Productions (United Artists), made a film titled *The Battle of Britain.* It was shot on various locations in England and in Spain. For the first time, the British tried to condense a very complex subject, for the English a deeply emotional event, into the framework of a two-hour movie. Adolf Galland joined the shooting as German consultant. It will always remain unexplainable to the aviation buff why the names, titles, markings and squadron insignia of the German fighter and bomber-units were changed. From time to time, thematic concepts and ideas of the English producers generated grave concern among the German consultants, resulting in periods of temporary discord. However, the filming was completed and it ended a success. After the September premieres in Cologne and London, as well as in October in the US and in Canada, in which AG and the British aces of the Battle of Britain participated, millions of spectators saw the film.

In 1970 the industry consultant fulfilled a further wish. He likes Spain, and he speaks the Spanish language fluently after his years of living in Argentina. He knew Spain and its people from his service with the Condor Legion. On the Costa Blanca he built a wonderful holiday home where he spends his vacations with his children and where his family and friends visit him and enjoy his hospitality.

In September 1971 Galland participated in the first Commonwealth Wartime Aircrew Reunion in Winnipeg, Canada. He was the only former enemy and simultaneously guest of honor of the Wartime Pilots and Observers Association. The speech which the former General of the Fighter Arm delivered to the audience of Commonwealth WW II aircrews was received with overwhelming applause. On that occasion, Adolf Galland and three other guests of honor were made honorary citizens by the City of Winnipeg.

In September 1970, Galland participated in Rudolf Woller's TV documentary, *When Fire Fell From the Sky*, dealing with the airwar over Germany. Galland gradually became a highly-regarded speaker at many clubs, associations, German and foreign military meetings, symposiums, etc. In January 1974 he participated in a wargame at the famous British Staff College in Sandhurst. The subject of this wargame, "Operation Sea Lion 1940," dealt with the planned German invasion of England.

In 1974 Galland bought an apartment in Bonn-Bad Godesberg, where his office is now located. Here, the author spent many hours - ably assisted by his splendid secretary, Mrs. Drinhausen, in preparation of this book.

Hunting, for Adolf Galland, is welcome relief from his hectic business schedule. Since his youth, he was an enthusiastic hunter and an excellent marksman thanks to his sharp eyesight and almost legendary reaction speed. He became the dominant figure during many hunting parties to which he was invited, and often he ends these days as the most successful of the hunters. It is a self-understood fact for Adolf Galland to dress his animals and to filet the game trophies himself.

Besides his business commitments, Galland stands as an historic link between the past and present. Lectures given at the NATO HQ, SHAPE, and NASA confirm this fact. This was especially documented on the occasion of the opening of the German hall at Hendon's RAF Museum near London, in December 1975. Adolf Galland was an invited guest. A long conversation with Prince Charles, the British successor to the throne, confirmed the high regard this German fighter ace enjoys in England. Forty years after the most horrible war which humanity has endured, Adolf Galland's popularity has not faded. He did not become a living monument, but a distinguished personality, who managed the change from a successful fighter pilot to successful leader of the fighter arm, and — after the disaster of World War II — managed the change from a military to a successful commercial career.

"Fame and tranquility do not go together" is his motto. He neither knows nor likes lethargy. He always left the slow ones behind and did not look back. He is a realist, but still a convinced idealist. He enjoys resistance, since it is a challenge for him. He accepted this challenge many years before and he always kept on acting accordingly during the 40 years that followed. Self-confident, decisive and often impatient — always one step ahead of the others, and sometimes even ahead of himself — he went his own long way. He accepted his past self-critically, and recognizes the advantages and responsibilities of the Democratic Government that he is determined to support and defend.

Adolf Galland, former General of Fighters — the "Capitano," the "Mufti" as his fellow pilots know him — became a connecting link between the fighter pilots of all nations. During the International Fighter Pilots Reunion at Munich in October 1979, fighter pilots of 12 nations met in an atmosphere of friendship and international comradeship. The presence of AG certainly attracted many of them to Munich.

Spring 1955 - Galland and his first wife visit the Heinkel factories at Stuttgart-Zuffenhausen. On the photo from left to right: S. Gunter, A. Galland, unknown, Prof. Ernst Heinkel, Truckenbrodt, Mrs. Galland, W. Gunter, K. Schwarzler and Seekatz.

While in Hannover in May 1957, Galland made his first supersonic flight aboard a British Hawker Hunter two-seater.

Each year since his return to Germany, Galland takes part in the traditional German air rally *(Deutschlandflug)*. In June 1957 his "vehicle" was a Piper PA-18.

In 1958 he became the winner of his class, flying a Klemm.

"Pips" Priller, the last *Kommodore* of JG-26, died unexpectedly on 20 May 1961. Many former members and friends of the fighter wing joined the funeral of the beloved wing commander.

At the grave-site are to be seen from the left: "Schorsch" Eder, Edu Neumann, Adolf Galland, Werner Schroer, F. Bohnmuller, Werner Andres and Theo Lindemann.

In 1961, Galland became Pilot of the Year, and later Honorary Life Member of the IOC. This massive trophy was presented to Galland as a visible sign of the esteem he enjoys among the members of the "International Order of Characters," a worldwide aviation organization.

Two Sikorskys, father and son, with Dr. Crane, the President and "brain" of the IOC. Igor Sikorsky was the late genial designer of famous aircraft; particularly the helicopter.

With a group of IOC-members

Adolf Galland and Sergei Sikorsky.

Besides flying and hunting, clay-pigeon shooting is another hobby of Galland's.

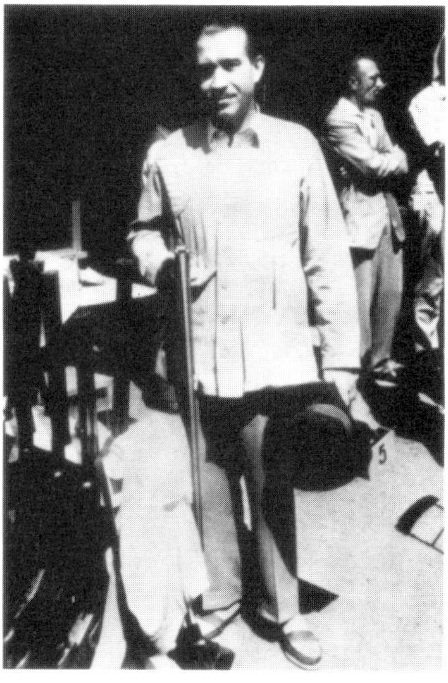

Hunting in the Eifel.

In the meantime, Galland was divorced from his first wife and married for the second time. Mrs. Galland in the middle of the photo.

20 years after the war, Galland meets the former *Kommodore* of JG-51 (Molders), Karlfried Nordmann. Both are talking to the President of the US Fighter Aces Association, at that time Jack Bradley.

Colonel Werner Molders' original award certificate for the oak leaves with swords is handed over to Werner Anders and Adolf Galland - both representing the German Fighter Pilots Association - by a USAF officer. Today, this certificate is displayed at the present JG-74 *Molders* headquarters in Neuberg/Donau.

Bonn-the Grand Ball of the Aviation Club of Germany. Adolf Galland surrounded by prominent friends with their ladies. From the left to the right: Major General Hrabak, Mrs. Hartmann, Colonel Erich Hartmann, Galland, Countess von Vitzthum, Mr. Becher, Miss Bleil and Mrs. Galland.

The former spokesman for the government, and later ambassador in London, Secretary of State von Hase and Mrs. von Hase are seen in a moment of relaxation.

The Grand Ball of Air Force Group South, in Kasrlsruhe was attended by many famous aerospace and political personalities. From the left: General Hannes Trautloft, Adolf Galland, Wing Commander Peter Townsend, German Minister of Defense Georg Leber, Prime Minister Filbinger and French General Massu.

The German air rally in June 1967. Two enthusiastic pilots form a team - Erich Hartmann and Adolf Galland. Galland's Beech Bonanza fought bravely. On the right, Wing Commander Robert Stanford-Tuck, a close friend of A.G. for many years.

"The Fat One" with the registration D-EHEX and the rally entry number 107 in the air.

Konstanz-May 1968. During a pilot's reunion, Galland takes a look at Lake Constance from the cockpit of a motor-glider.

On 7 November 1966, something happened which gave Galland a deep inner happiness . . . the birth of a son, Andreas-Hubertus. In the photo, on the right: the "Flying Father" Schulte, who celebrated the baptism. On 29 July 1969, daughter Alexandra-Isabelle was born. Adolf Galland is proud of his children and loves both of them gently.

The original birth-announcements were drawn by Sergei Sikorsky.

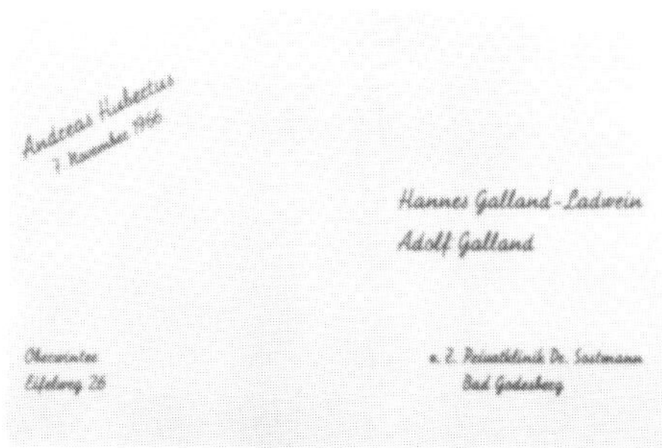

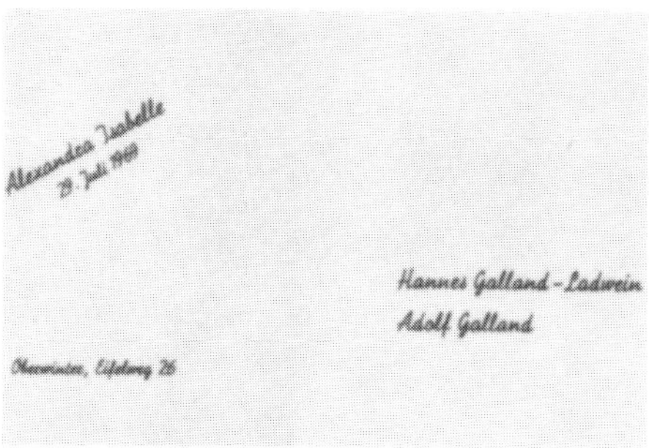

Celebrating the "happy event," many former fighter pilots found their way to the Galland house at Oberwinter. Some decades ago they fought together, or even against each other and registered a total of 1,127 air victories. On the photo from the left: Steinhoff, Hartmann, Barkhorn, Falck, Stanford-Tuck (RAF), Hrabak, Powell (RAF), Lindemann, Galland, Andres and Schopfel.

An American fighter pilot, Edward H. Sims, wrote a book titled *The Fighter Pilots - Former Enemies,* and presents the first copies. From the left: Sims, Steinhoff, Stanford-Tuck, Galland and Hartmann.

Former enemies - Stanford-Tuck and Galland - are close friends today. Here they are seen while pheasant hunting in England.

Mr. and Mrs. Galland in their best mood. No wonder, they are sniffing airport air at the Baden-Baden Airfield.

In November 1969, the Community College of Trier organized an unusual historical forum in which General Chuck Yeager and Adolf Galland participated. Yeager, a fighter ace in World War II, was the first pilot to break the sound barrier.

Galland delivered a lecture to the officers of a US fighter wing at Spangdahlem in the Eifel.

He also delivered a speech at the USAF Base in Phalsbourg, to fighter pilots on "Sabre Night."

In March 1968, Galland met his close friend "Tonius" Weiler, member of the Board of Directors of the Gerling Trust, and Dr. F.W. Christians, speaker of the Board of Directors of the Deutsche Bank at the Bonn-Hangelar airport to discuss the crop-spraying market.

March 1969 in the Sudan. As Chairman of the Board of Directors of Air Lloyd Deutsche Helicopter Service Company, Galland inaugurated a helicopter pilots school. He is welcomed by the Sudanese Minister of Agriculture on the Civil Airport in Khartoum.

A passionate hunter such as Galland does not miss the chance for a safari. The photo was made after a successful hunt on the prairie of southern Sudan.

1967 - 1968. Galland participated as consultant in the shooting of the film *The Battle of Britain.* The British side was represented, among others, by Robert Stanford-Tuck. The film, which became a big success, was produced mainly in England. However, location shots were also made in Spain. It was here in Seville where AG made his final Me-109 flight. He used one of the a/c with Rolls-Royce Merlin engines license-produced in Spain. A rather uncommon photo for the experts.

A group photo with the actors. From left to right: Heinz Riess, nearly the same build as Goring; Manfred Reddemann as Major Falcke (representing Adolf Galland), Galland; an actor (name unknown) representing a German fighter pilot; Paul Neuhaus as Major Fohn (representing Werner Molders). Wilfried van Aacken as *Jafu 2,* General Osterkamp, and the very lively "Uncle Theo" Osterkamp at that time. The change of the names of the represented persons led to some friction in the beginning, but an agreement was reached later on.

In September 1969 the German Premiere of the film with the title *The Battle of Britain (Die Luftschlact um England)* took place. Naturally, one finds AG as one of the honored guests as well as Lieutenant General Steinhoff, CIC of the new German Air Force, and Brigadier General Dieter Hrabak in the right corner.

Galland promoted the film in various TV interviews. In the foreground a model of the Merlin-powered Me-109. The talk show was made by German Television in Hamburg for its program dealing with current events.

Aerial photo of the Galland house after its final enlargement. The splendid property is located on the Rhine hills at Oberwinter. The restless Galland lives here and enjoys a few moments of rest after his hectic working days.

Here, in this wonderful trophy-hall in the right wing of his house, Galland welcomes his guests. The comfortable atmosphere is suitable for long talks in front of the big fireplace. In this hall the other portrait (made in 1942) finds its special place. It shows the former *Kommodore* Adolf Galland without a cigar, as specifically ordered by Hitler.

In September 1970 Galland was, for the first time, a guest of honor at the Commonwealth Wartime Aircrew Reunion in Winnipeg. Famous fighter pilots of other nations were also invited. In the second row from the right: Air Vice-Marshal Johnnie Johnson from England; Johnny Fauquier from Canada; Sir Douglas Bader from England and Adolf Galland.

Beside the other three special guests, the former enemy was awarded with an honorary citizenship by the town of Winnipeg. For Galland, a deeply appreciated gesture.

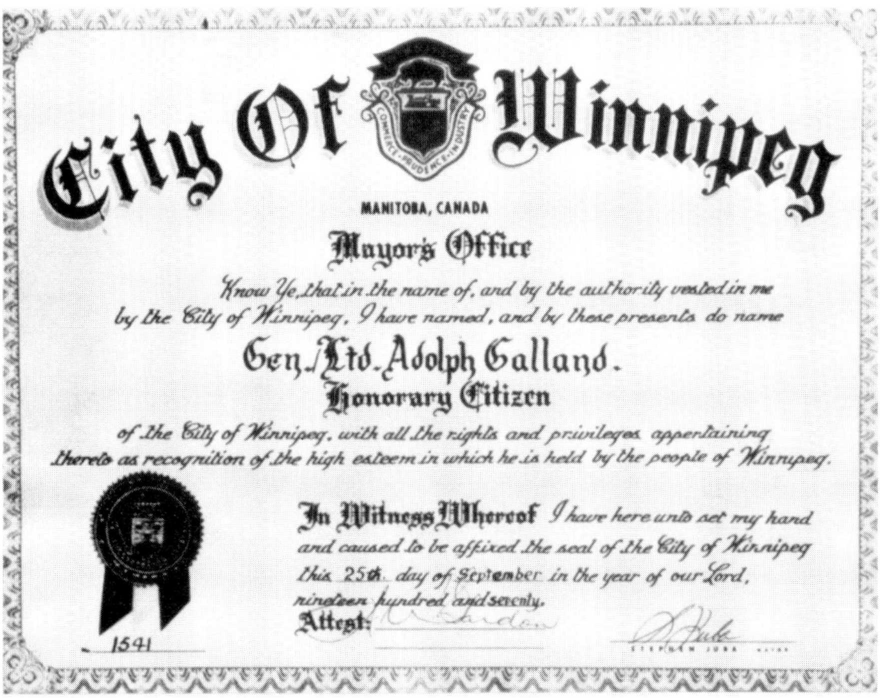

City Of Winnipeg

MANITOBA, CANADA

Mayor's Office

Know Ye, that in the name of, and by the authority vested in me by the City of Winnipeg, I have named, and by these presents do name

Gen. Ltd. Adolph Galland.

Honorary Citizen

of the City of Winnipeg, with all the rights and privileges appertaining thereto as recognition of the high esteem in which he is held by the people of Winnipeg.

In Witness Whereof I have here unto set my hand and caused to be affixed the seal of the City of Winnipeg this 25th day of September in the year of our Lord, nineteen hundred and seventy.

Attest:

1541

STEPHEN JUBA MAYOR

In March 1972 Galland became 60 and many guests from Germany and abroad came to congratulate him on his birthday. On the group photo standing from left to right: Rodel, Dr. Roos, Schopfel, Lindemann, Stanford-Tuck, Galland, Kuhlmay, Osterkamp, Brustellin, Krupinski, Rall, Schroer. Strumpell and on the ground Neumann and Falck.

Adolf Galland celebrating his birthday with his friend Edu Neumann and Galland's son, Andreas-Hubertus, called "Andus."

The First Communion of Andreas-Hubertus was another opportunity for a celebration, but this time only with family members. How proud the parents are can easily be seen.

Others are also getting older; Prof. Messerschmitt celebrates his 70th birthday. One of the gratulants is Adolf Galland. The photo was made during the ceremony in honor of Prof. Messerschmitt in the German Museum in Munich.

A new rendezvous with an Me-262. In 1974 - on a business trip to Australia - Galland visited the RAAF Station Point Cook in Victoria. Beside several other German warcraft, he found a well-preserved Me-262. Air Commodore A. Tonkin proudly shows his guests the rarity from past days.

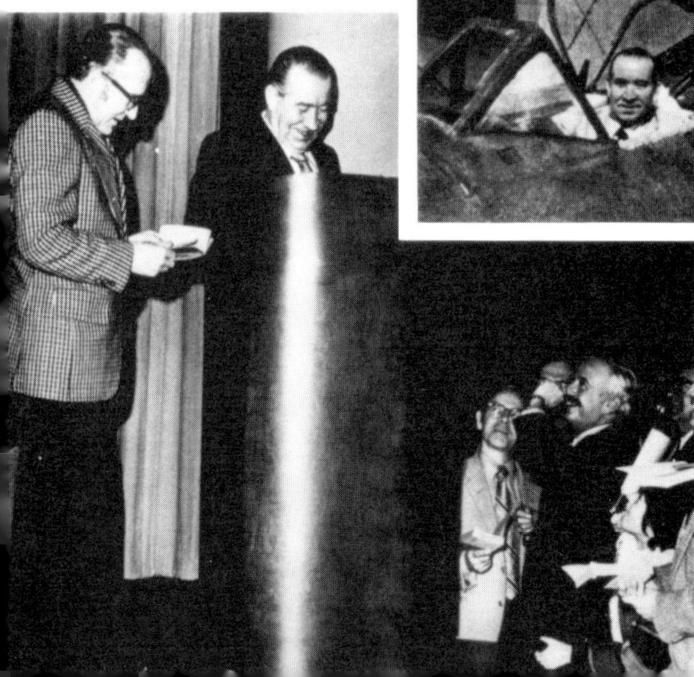

In February 1975 Galland gave a lecture at the War Museum in Ottawa on the subject of "The Channel Dash- the breakout of the heavy German battleships," 12 and 13 February 1942. Following this, he fulfilled the desire of his fans for autographs and signatures in his book.

"To Your health, my dear sirs!" Adolf Galland and two pioneers of aerospace, Dr. Kurt Debus (in the middle), who was director of the Kennedy Space Center for decades, and Wolfgang von Gronau who became famous in aviation history with long-distance flights in the Dornier "Whale" flying boats.

Former German Minister of Economy Schiller and his Secretary of State at that time, Schellhorn, listen with attention to Galland's comments. Adolf Galland, a successful businessman, with constant contacts with economic experts around the world, has a special feeling for this subject.

Galland with his Beech Bonanza "The Fat One" on the Air Lloyd Base. In 1963 Galland became chairman of the board of directors of this firm.

Before taking off the pilot concentrates, and human being and aircraft become one.

Mrs. Heidi Horn, Galland's co-pilot for many years, studies the charts. Mrs. Horn, an active pilot, became Galland's wife early in 1984.

In December 1975 Prince Charles opened the RAF Museum at Hendon near London. Prince Charles, also an RAF pilot, is talking to the German guest of honor, Adolf Galland. In the middle Stanford-Tuck, Galland's friend for many years.

Two friends, standing in front of an Me-109 in the RAF Museum. The models which both hold are copies of the planes in which each flew against the other in earlier times.

Wittmund 1975 - Galland has landed with "The Fat One." Only during the Richthofen Meeting in Wittmund are private planes permitted at the air force base.

The Commodore of JG-71 *Richthofen,* Colonel Rentel, welcomes pilots of the three Richthofen Fighter Wing generations.

The technical equipment of today's air forces is not unknown to Galland. Here he is seen with Brigadier General Hans Drebing, head of German Army Aviation in the cockpit of a CH-53 helicopter simulator.

October 1975 in Stolberg - Reception with CAE Electronics. CAE's manager, Mr. Fritz K. Stock, standing next to Mrs. Heidi Horn-Galland.

1976 - Meeting of the "Old Eagles" in Dusseldorf. A happy gathering after an uninhibited welcome to Germany's most famous lady-pilot, flight-captain Hanna Reitsch. In the background the good old "Antie Ju" (Junkers Ju-52).

Once again, in February 1975, in Ottawa Galland gives a lecture on the Channel Dash - the breakout of the heavy German battleships in February 1942 - at the University of Norwich in Northfield, Vermont.

"The Fat One," Galland's Beech Bonanza is stationed at Bonn-Hangelar airfield. From here he takes off for business-trips within Europe and for numerous goodwill appearances.

England - 1976. The Billericay Squadron of the RAF celebrates a festive dinner in Hornchurch, Essex on the occasion of the 35th anniversary of the Battle of Britain. From the left: Wing Commander Alick Grant, Mrs. Grant, AG, Mrs. Heidi Horn-Galland, Wing Commander Robert Stanford-Tuck, Mrs. Tuck and other invited guests.

In September of the same year Galland again joined the Wartime Aircrew Reunion in Winnipeg. Many other famous guests of honor represented various air forces: Francis "Gabby" Gabreski, the top living US fighter ace; General Doolittle, who led the first bombers over Tokyo, taking off from the aircraft carrier *Hornet* to hit targets considered invulnerable by the Japanese. In the second row are Lt. Col. Kilpatrick, President, Officers Mess/Winnipeg; Air Vice-Marshal J.E. (Johnnie) Johnson; Air-Chief Marshal Sir Dennis Smallwood; Col. M. Gates, base commander, Winnipeg; M.G. Boak, O.B. E., Secretary General RAF Association. In the front line: Col. F.S. Gabreski-USA; Lt. Gen. W.C. Carr, Commander, Air Command, C.F.; Group Captain T. White, RNZAF; Air Commodore J. Fauquier, RCAF; Capt. A. Whitehouse, Royal Flying Corps (WW I); Galland; Group Captain Sir Douglas Bader.

On behalf of the German Fighter Pilots Association, Adolf Galland hands over a generous contribution to his Canadian hosts for a war monument they plan to erect.

Former fighter pilots swapping "war stories."

Galland shows Douglas Bader details of a Me-109 Model.

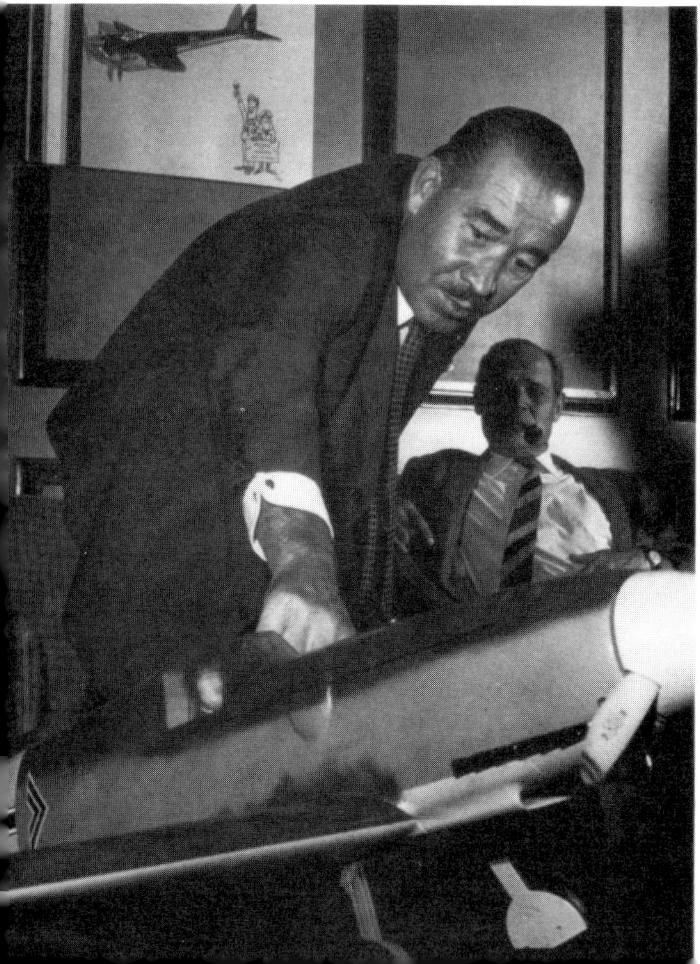

The proud father with his children: son Andreas-Hubertus and daughter Alexandra-Isabelle, who continue a warm relationship with their father after the divorce of the parents in 1973. The photo below: Galland with his children and their friend in front of "The Fat One."

Adolf Galland in his office in Bonn-Bad Godesberg in July 1977. The high-backed chair he is sitting in, has its own history: Once upon a time the Western Allied High Commissioners sat in it while holding their meetings on the Petersberg near Bonn. The commissioners were the executive organ of the occupation powers after WW II.

September 1967 - a visit to Prof. Messerschmitt. While on holiday in Spain, a chance was found to visit the great old pioneer of German aviation in his country home near Marbella. From the left: Galland, Mrs. Horn-Galland, Schmidt-Lossberg, Prof. Messerschmitt and Mrs. Auert.

Carefree holidays in Spain. Old friends visit Galland in his house: Anton Weiler, Gotthard Handrick and Edu Neumann. It is certain that another forgotten adventure from the past was again rediscovered.

On the terrace of his house with Louis Wienken and "Tonius" Weiler. Wienken was working as an interpreter in Galland's squadron during the civil war in Spain.

Despite his business engagements and social commitments, Adolf Galland does not forget hunting. It remains his most favorite hobby. In Hungary in September of 1967, he shot this huge 16-point stag.

Galland together with his gamekeeper, Kalman, after a successful hunt.

A large stag is carried home.

On a hunting trip in the Eifel; Galland and Stanford-Tuck are sighting in their rifles.

In December 1977 Galland and his son Andreas-Hubertus join a hunt in Oberwinter.

Photo at left: After the hunt.

Galland surrounded by members of the Australian Pathfinders Association on the occasion of their visit to Munich in July 1978. Galland, General (ret.) Barkhorn and Colonel (ret.) Falck are answering requests for autographs on the Neureuther Alm.

February 1978 in London. Adolf Galland, Stanford-Tuck and the famous aviation Artist, Frank Wootton, signing prints of the painting "Achtung Spitfire." Part of the proceeds gained from the sale of 850 limited edition prints was used to expand the Air Force Museum at Hendon.

In October of the same year, the RAF Club in London hosted a reception on the occasion of the introduction of the painting "Bader Bale Out." (In the background). From the left: R. Stanford-Tuck, Sir Denis Crowley-Milling, Wing Commander H. Dundas, Sir John Grandy, Sir Douglas Bader, Wing Commander P. Barthrop, Galland, Sir B. Heath, P. Thorn, Frank Wootton and Group Commander B. Kingcome.

Oldtimer Aircraft Meeting in August 1978 in Bex near Montreux-Switzerland. The guests of honor (who acted as the judges) being driven to their positions, (from the left) Geoffrey Page, Galland, Stanford-Tuck and Douglas Bader.

Adolf Galland in the cockpit of a Spitfire ready for takeoff. Now it is years too late for him, sitting in the Spitfire he so often desired to fly. The faces of his English friends seem to confirm this.

Galland's 65th birthday was celebrated on 19 March 1977 in the Redoubt in Bad Godesberg, hosted by the insurance company Gerling Trust. Among the hundreds of guests are ten prominent Commodores of the former Luftwaffe: from the left: W. Falck, NJG-1; F. Obleser, CIC of the GAF in 1977; W. Schroer, JG-27; J. Steinhoff, JG-7; Galland; D. Hrabak, JG-54; G. Rodel, JG-27; Dr. H. Lange, JG-51; "Assi" Hahn, II/JG-54; G. Schopfel, JG-6.

Also present on that occasion were former Generals Wust, Limberg and Obleser.

Daughter Alexandra-Isabelle wished for a violin as her First Communion gift. Now she tries the instrument in the presence of her father.

Wim Thoelke - former sports announcer and presently a prominent talk-show host - has been Galland's friend for many years. Thoelke is an enthusiastic pilot and also owns a Bonanza. Both pilots have sufficient subjects to talk about while meeting at the buffet.

The morning after the 1978 Luftwaffe Ball the following gentlemen met at Galland's house for a hang-over-breakfast: from the left: Krupinski, Galland, Falck, Hrabak, Rall and Obleser.

Senator Willy Roder, celerating his 75th birthday. Adolf Galland came to Egelsbach, where Roder lived to congratulate his friend.

International Fighter Pilots Meeting in Munich, October 1979. Fourteen nations were represented and former enemies are now friends. Over the years, Galland did his share to make this event possible. From the left: Barkhorn, Page (RAF), Galland, Bader (RAF), Hartmann, Stanford-Tuck (RAF) and Rall.

In March 1980 Galland's former university comrades of many years ago meet in Oberwinter. The photo was made in Galland's pilot's bar.

May 1980 in Dublin. After a lecture, Galland was the guest of the commander of the aviation division.

In September 1980, Galland participated for the third time in the Commonwealth Aircrew Reunion in Winnipeg as guest of honor.

A successful elk hunt in the Yukon Territory in Canada, in September 1980.

A group photo following a banquet given at the invitation of Bill Bettis in his outstanding restaurant in Santa Ana, California.

In the front row sitting at the table from left: Dr. Ferdie Pacheco; Larry Forester; Bill Bettis; Leigh Vance; James Brooks; Galland; Virginia Bader; Bill Ackermann; Robert DeHaven. Standing behind from the left: Kirk Armistead; Curtis LeMay; Raymond F. Toliver; Russ Schleeh; Al Osequera; R.G. Smith; Duke Vincent; Norma Bert; Zeke Cormier; Jay Hubbard; Robert Stanford-Tuck.

Visiting General Dynamics' plant in Fort Worth, Texas in October 1980, Galland and Robert Stanford-Tuck were briefed by the company's by the company's chief pilot, Neil R. Anderson, about the cockpit of the highly sophisticated F-16.

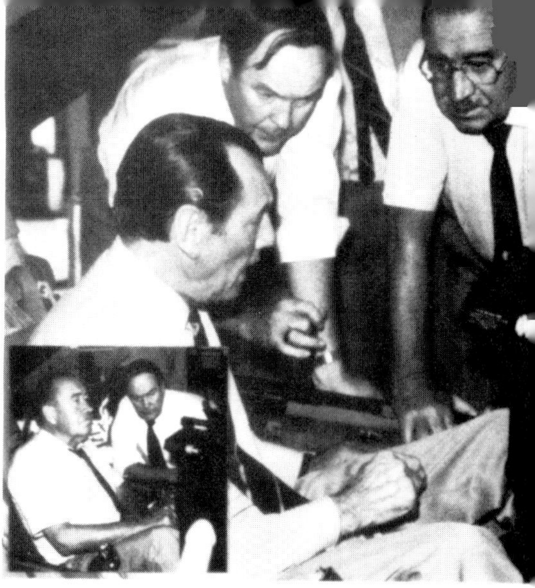

The Confederate Air Force, a well-known association of aviators, technicians and supporters, spread across the United States, is dedicated to the reconstruction, maintenance and flight demonstration of WW II planes. Stanford-Tuck and Galland become honorary members. Like all members, they are awarded the rank of colonel. This took place in October 1980 on the occasion of a three-day airshow in Harlingen, Texas.

The group clearly shows how rough life is while on duty with the C.A.F.

In October 1980 Adolf Galland was reunited with, among others, his very valuable over-and-under skeet shotguns which were brought to the US as war booty. The return of the guns was made possible by the generosity of wealthy Americans. Galland will always be thankful to Robert R. Crow and Joe Buffer.

Here, General Doolittle is seen testing one of Galland's guns in Santa Ana near Los Angeles.

The very talented organizer, Virginia Bader (Fine Arts Ltd.) and Adolf Galland make one of their frequent visits, in February 1981, to the National Air and Space Museum in Washington, D.C.

Adolf Galland is also welcome at the Air Force Museum, Wright Patterson Air Force Base in Ohio. Here, in March 1982 he delivered a speech.

19 March, 1983 was of special importance for Galland. On that occasion he celebrated his 70th birthday by inviting fighter pilots and business friends to a reception and a gala dinner at the Hotel Exelsior in Cologne. Here, also Galland is an excellent host.

A visit to his Houston, Texas friend, John Henry Kirby III, on Easter 1982. Kirby proudly demonstrates his restored Bucker 133 *Jungmeister.*

Galland in the cockpit of a restored Me-109K which was flown during the Hannover Air Show in April 1982.

On 17 May 1983, the two historians, Ray Toliver and Trevor Constable, met in Galland's office with the author of this book, Werner Held.

On the occasion of the visit of the American historians Toliver and Constable, who were working on Galland's biography, a small fighter pilots' meeting was arranged in Galland's house at Oberwinter. Wing Commander (ret.) Robert Stanford-Tuck and Wing Commander Alick Grant came from England. The President of the German Fighter Pilots Association, Anton Weiler, presented Robert Stanford-Tuck with an honorary membership certificate in the Association. We see a smiling host surrounded by equally-relaxed guests. From the left: Stammberger, Schopfel, Grasser, Dr. Lange, Jabs, Krupinski, Galland, Trautloft, Toliver, Hrabak, Constable, Stanford-Tuck, Grant, Schmoller-Haldy, Rall.

Gathering of the generals. On the occasion of the funeral of Major General Gerhard Barkhorn and his wife on 14 January 1983 at Tegernsee, from left to right: Lt. General Jorg Kuebart, Lt. Gen. Friedrich Obleser, Galland, Lt. General Fritz Wegner, and Lt. General Eberhard Eimler.

Both these photos clearly show the happy mood of two old soldiers visiting their former boss on 25 June 1983 at his house in Oberwinter. One was Galland's former crew chief during the whole war, Gerhard Meyer (left) and his armourer, Heinrich Olemotz.

How fast the years pass by can easily be observed by watching ones' own children grow. Here Andreas-Hubertus and Alexandra-Isabelle with their proud father.

Heidi and Adolf Galland at their home at Oberwinter in the morning of their wedding-day, 10th February 1984.

Exactly one month later a wedding reception was given at Oberwinter. The photo shows the Gallands with their children, from the left: Alexandra Galland, Andreas Galland, Claudia Hengel, Marco Linsenmann.

Gathering of fighter pilots on the occasion of the wedding reception: From the left to the right: J. Burschgens, J. Mohn, Editor of Jagerblatt, H. Schmoller-Haldy, Dr. H. Lange, Lt. General ret. F. Obleser, Lt. General ret. G. Limberg, W. Bartels, Lt. General ret. W. Panitzki, Lt. General ret. G. Rall, Th. Lindemann, Mrs. Galland, A. Galland, W. Falck, F. Losigkeit, J. Jabs, Major General ret. D. Hrabak, Brig. General ret. G. Rodel, sitting from the left: Major General ret. H.U. Flade, the late W. Schroer, Major General ret. W. Krupinski, Edu Neumann and sitting on the ground, Anton Weiler, President of Fighter Pilots Association.

In May of the same year Heidi joins her husband during a symposium "Battle of the Skies - the Luftwaffe" at the Waverly Hotel in Atlanta. The other three gentlemen next to A. Galland are from the left: Lt. General ret. Gunther Rall, General ret. Johannes Steinhoff and Major General ret. Walter Krupinski.

Adolf Galland and Douglas Champlin with the Champlin Musuem's Bf-109E at Mesa, Arizona in May 1984. The occasion was the annual meeting of the American Fighter Aces Association.